Understanding
Your
Dog

12

Understanding Your Dog

Barbara Sykes

The Crowood Press

First published in 2001 by
The Crowood Press Ltd
Ramsbury, Marlborough
Wiltshire SN8 2HR

www.crowood.com

Paperbook edition 2007

© Barbara Sykes 2001

British Library Cataloguing-in-Publication Data
A catalogue record for this book is available from the British
Library.

ISBN 978 1 86126 941 6

Photographs by Malcolm and Maureen Merone, Betty Duggan
and the author

Line illustrations by Caroline Simpson and David Fisher

Typeset by Jean Cussons Typesetting, Diss, Norfolk

Printed and bound in Spain by GraphyCems

Contents

Acknowledgements

I would like to give a special thank you to Maureen Merone, who has patiently listened to my extended telephone calls and has read and reread copies, and amended copies, of the manuscript to enable her to get a feel for the kinds of photograph we needed. Without Malcolm and Maureen's expertise with a camera and their willingness to take photographs from all angles, which have involved their lying for lengths of time in long grass and water, our photographs would not tell a story.

I would also like to thank Caroline Simpson; I appreciate the time she spent reading, studying and reproducing my ideas in graphics so clearly. I am also grateful to the members of the CWD dog training club Southport who either participated in or assisted with the photographs, to the proprietors of The Springs Boarding Kennels, Eldwick, Bradford, and to everyone who patiently allowed an invasion of their privacy while we photographed their dogs. And grateful thanks to Rocky, Fudge, Twix, Texas, Eric, Gemma and Floss, our cover dogs, for their patience and to their handlers Andrea Little, Greta Cheetham, Jane Halsall and Maureen Merone.

Introduction

This book is not aimed at any specific form of training; it is a journey into the dog's mind, its instincts and its perception of life. It does not matter whether you are training for one of the disciplines or your dog is a pet, whether you have a small dog or a large one; the more you know about its mind, what it is thinking and how it communicates the easier training will be.

Throughout these pages there are photographs depicting the dog's-eye view and the human's-eye view. We all know that a dog does not see the world from our height, but we are often guilty of not realizing just what the dog really does, or rather does not see.

Some readers may be surprised that I actually state that it is acceptable for a dog to sleep upstairs or even in the bedroom, but I am not advocating that everyone who reads the book should promptly take their dog to bed with them. It is a long journey of understanding and training that enables a dog and its handler to be able to enjoy such freedom and the more freedom a dog has the more rules it must obey.

All dogs have similar instincts, so this book deals with the small, the medium and the large, rather than with specific breeds; there has been no preference given to breeds other than what was needed for each photograph, and these have all been taken to tell their own story.

Young dogs are like young children: they learn through recognition and instinct, and we teach a child one language and one culture before we begin feeding it with further information. If we learn our dog's language it is easier to communicate with and to teach the animal; but above all we must allow dogs to recognize what they are. They are dogs and if we do not help them to recognize dog behaviour and instincts they will never have an identity, for, as dear as they may be to us, they will never be human beings and neither should we want them to be. They are free spirits, with thoughts, opinions and a sense of humour, so enjoy finding out about them, channelling their natural instincts and developing their characters. This book is not aimed at teaching you how to train your dog for any specific purpose; it is aimed at helping you to understand your dog and to teach it good manners to enable you to go forward into any form of training you wish. But above all it is intended to help you to understand and to identify with the dog in your life.

Free Spirits

Free of spirit, light of foot,
Loyal and trusting, faithful to the end.
Don't try to change him, be proud of what he is.
He is not just a dog,
He is your best friend

Wonderful eyes that search for you,
Beseeching you to come.
A heart that gives, never takes
And beats for you alone.
Make understanding him your goal,
And in those faithful eyes
You will see his very soul.

For he is the one friend
Who accepts you for what you are,
Forgives you for what you are not,
And even when he is gone
Will still be with you till the end.

B. S.

CHAPTER 1

The Dog for You

Training a dog need not be difficult and it is only as complicated as we wish to make it. Most dogs have a straightforward approach to life and humans often confuse them by failing to understand their language and by making their training complicated. There is a saying that a little learning may be a dangerous thing, but sometimes a human being can make the training difficult by learning too much. The main criteria for training a dog are common sense and understanding; all the dog training and all the dog psychology in the world will not help you if you do not understand your dog and do not have empathy with it. The words 'dog training' are easy to understand – they are self-explanatory, meaning 'to train a dog'. The word psychology, be it human or canine, conjures up something a little more complicated, yet it means simply 'to study the mind'. The members of a close-knit family will take the time and trouble to study one another; parents and teachers will endeavour to find the best form of communication by which to teach children, they each try to understand what the other is thinking. Your dog's behaviour is a result of its thought processes. No matter how simple these processes are it is still the result of a working mind and as such you should be able, with a little thought and effort, to gain access to this 'inside information', thus enabling you to have a better understanding of your dog and how to train him.

Before you can start to gain this access to the information inside your dog's head you need to know a little about his background. If you know something about his immediate ancestors you will know where he gets his markings and certain characteristics from; if you delve a little deeper you will find certain traits being handed down over the generations, as with humans. So if we go back to the early development of the dog we know today, we can learn a lot about their behaviour patterns and how to educate them.

Just as modern man has evolved from prehistoric man, so has the modern dog evolved from its hunting, predatorial ancestors. To be able to understand and relate to the modern dog we need to understand and even think like the hunting pack dog. Of course, man, who is never content and always striving to 'improve' upon nature, has over the years interfered with certain breeds of dog, changing their appearance and, in some instances, subduing their natural instincts. Indeed, there are breeds of dogs to be found today that were no-where to be seen a little over a century ago, the result of man's 'manufacturing' a new breed from two or more originals.

The pug is believed to be a miniature

descendant of the prehistoric dog and from this breed we can see some similarity to some of today's toy breeds. The chihuahua is descended, through the Aztec sacred dog, from a Spanish original and is related to the papillon, and the poodle need not settle for being only 'part' working dog as he was originally used for working sheep and water fowl. Today we have variations of the poodle breed, but if we look closely at the brown poodle we can see the similarity between it and the Irish water spaniel. In fact, many of today's true breeds are a result of cross-breeding through the centuries, and, although this has produced variations of certain breeds and in some cases an entirely new breed of dog, it is not always for the better. For, when a degree of success is evident in one aspect of breeding, a 'flaw' or omission may occur that may or may not have been planned. For example, when breeding for one particular reason, be it for appearance, improvement or to produce a new breed, there is no guarantee that the result will have all the qualities of the original. The miniature poodle could not and would not be expected to herd sheep and work as the French poodle used to, and how many Sealyham owners can imagine their dog out hunting! Many of today's breeds no longer have the instincts of their predecessors and the toy breeds do not usually pose the same training and behavioural problems of the larger breeds. However, large or small, pure breed or not, handlers need to be able to communicate with their dogs. Prevention is better than cure and a 'problem' or misunderstood dog is not a happy one; unhappy dogs make their caring owners unhappy too as they strive to find a solution.

Natural Instincts

The need to understand the instincts of the dogs in their pack days and to be able to relate them to today is important to the well-being of any breed. For to understand the mind of a dog, regardless of its size or breed, not only makes training easier but also makes the sharing of your life with that same dog more interesting. This book is about understanding what is going on in the mind of your dog.

When you ask your dog to do something, its mind begins to work, it responds to the tone of your voice, the request you made and decides whether it intends to take notice of you. But before you made this contact with your dog, whether by voice or body language, it was by no means in a dormant state. It may not have been following the human train of thought – 'Did I leave the electricity on and what shall we have for supper?' – but nevertheless its mind would still be active. If we look at a dog in its original form, as a pack dog, it will be constantly using its brain; most of the time it will be on its guard, it will also be on the lookout for food, a mate, water, somewhere to sleep. All are actions that require some degree of thought; all are necessary to its existence. Left to its own devices, a dog will usually work things out for itself; it will find something to play with, something to chew, it will sleep when it is tired and will amuse itself when awake, finding amusement or making mischief to suit itself.

When we take a dog into our home we take away its ability for freethinking; no matter how caring we are, our dogs must live their lives in the way that we want them to. In the wild they would not be on chains, neither would they be sleeping in

Dogs are capable of making their own amusement; they need to be able to use their imagination, but they must be educated how to harness their instincts. Skye will spend hours tracking and digging for moles but she knows she must not chase nor use her teeth, so she never catches one.

a 'designer' bed; they would not be wearing a collar and they most certainly would not have someone attached to a lead. Their food would be of their choosing (how often do we reprimand our dogs for unsavoury eating habits?) and they would have access to natural herbage; they would not be chasing balls, chewing squeaky toys or flying through the air to catch a Frisbee. When out with the pack leader a dog would not be walking slightly ahead with its head twisted around looking up into the leader's face; it would be in its pack position – behind the leader. We are human and we take a dog into our lives for our own benefit; it may be for guarding, companionship, one of the many disciplines or for work. But whatever the lifestyle, we impose our human thoughts and way of life on to our dogs. For this reason we owe it to them to try to understand them and to communicate in

a way that they can recognize, in their own language.

This does not mean that human 'games' are wrong for your dog; it simply means that they are more fun for both human and dog if played according to the dog's natural understanding. For example, if a human hides a ball for the dog to seek, more often than not they are encouraging the dog with excited noises, gestures and higher than normal voice tones, often using words the dog has not heard before.

All this encourages the dog to be excited; it loses track of what it is doing; often barks and yaps and depends on the human to help it to seek. It is not using its natural thinking process. If, after showing the dog the ball, the human then hides it and stands quietly back, with no indication to the dog of what to do, it will start to think. It may only be wondering what to do next, but at least it is thinking,

The Newfoundland, renowned for its prowess in water, is not only a very large breed but its coat is capable of resisting water and therefore has special needs as regards grooming.

and in the natural dog world it would be able to track down moles, mice, and other delicacies by using its instincts and its brain, and all would be done quietly. All dogs have a natural intelligence and instincts; it is up to us to develop these skills, not allow them to lie dormant, nor to over-stimulate them to the point of hysteria. A great responsibility but such fun.

Before anyone takes a dog into his or her life the new owner will need to ask him or herself many questions; but are they the right questions? The main three facts to consider are: what have you to offer a dog? What do you expect from a dog? What breed would you prefer? All three are interlinked, and – notice the question – which breed would you *prefer* and not which breed do you intend to *have*? Why are these interlinked? First let us give a brief outline of each link.

What Have You to Offer a Dog?

We know that a dog needs exercise, feeding, grooming, somewhere to sleep and general care and attention; it would be pointless even to consider owning a dog if you could not provide such general care. But some breeds need more special attention than others do. Can you provide a dog with only these basic considerations, or can, and are you prepared, to offer more?

What Do You Expect from Your Dog?

Are you expecting your dog to be a companion or a working dog? Will you be competitive with it and if so with which sport? Are you hoping your dog will be a guard for your home? How many members are there in your family inter-

This small, fluffy bundle may not be happy 'fell walking' nor as a farm dog, and even if it has a ferocious bark for its size it will not be a deterrent for a determined intruder, but Hollie is an ideal candidate for a small house.

ested in sharing their life with a dog and are any of these small children?

Which Breed Do You Prefer?

Most people have a favourite breed, for some it is a small, fluffy bundle, for others it may be a large, powerful, hunting type. The first would not be suitable for fell walkers and working, and the second would be far too strong for someone frail or unable to commit himself or herself to plenty of daily exercise.

If we look closely at these three questions we can see how they link together, each answer being dependent on the other two. First of all you must consider your own lifestyle; what kind of a life you lead, how much free time you may have and the needs and wishes of other members of your family. There are many and varied breeds of dog, and the one you would really like to share your life with may not be the best breed to share your lifestyle. Remember that not choosing the breed of your first choice does not mean

that you are opting for second best; it means that you are choosing the best breed for you at that particular time. If you live on your own in an isolated house and you feel that you would be more secure with a dog which could bark a warning to strangers and would-be intruders, you would be defeating your object by acquiring one of the toy breeds. With the best will in the world, and no matter how aggressive a small breed may seem to be, it will not be a very convincing deterrent to intruders. Consider the dog too, for it will be trying to defend itself as well as its territory. A large dog does not need to be aggressive, the depth of the bark and the size of the dog are deterrent enough, even if it is likely to lick an intruder to death!

If you lead a busy life and the time you have available for exercising your dog is limited, it would be foolish to have a breed renowned for its needing plenty of exercise. If you wish to try your hand at competitive dog handling by training for

A large breed of dog can be a deterrent for unwelcome visitors just by its size and bark, but dogs such as Rex need plenty of exercise and mental stimulation.

Although Harry is a working breed he is not a sheepdog, and if he were to recognize sheep as part of his 'game plan' his instinct would be to chase rather than to herd them.

one of the sports, you will need to make sure that the breed you choose is equipped for the sport or sports of your choice. Although there is rarely a hard and fast rule as to which dog should compete at which sport, you would not think of entering a toy breed in a sheepdog trial, where the predominant breed is the Border Collie, but you may consider a Beardie. Similarly, any of the sports involving gun work will need a dog bred to the gun and a Border Collie would often fight shy of this, but a Springer Spaniel could be in its element. You will find few restrictions in agility, for, although some breeds are better able to jump at speed than others, there are usually classes, as in obedience, to suit all breeds. If you think your interests will lie in the show ring you will have to put much forethought into choosing your dog, because, for instance, its conformation,

colouring and height, must meet the standard for its particular breed.

If you have a luxury home with deep pile carpets and you intend to have a dog living inside the house, it would be wise to choose a breed with a fairly short, dark coat and not one that is constantly loosing hair. If your dog is going to live inside be cautious of the very large breeds – you can soon lose a table full of crockery with one wag of the tail. If you have a large garden or a small paddock with plenty of exercise area and possibly a shed you wish to use as an outside dog run, you will need something hardier than a miniature or toy breed. If you want your dog for work you will not have a varied choice of breed and the chances are that you will know exactly what you want and where to get it. Certain considerations must still be applied; for example, many working dogs are so enthusiastic with

Not all dogs are instinctively suited to living with other pets, so if your dog is of a working breed it must be taught to harness its instincts. Hope's natural instinct is to herd so he practises his skills on Tia the cat, but as he has never been allowed to chase, it develops into a harmless game.

their employment that they do not take kindly to small hands and high-pitched laughter or screaming. If you have, or live near children, and bearing in mind that other people's children are not always as 'dog conversant' as your own, you need to make sure that you can provide your dog with a 'safe house'. This is a golden rule for all dogs whether work or companion. Do you already have a dog or other pets? Not all dogs take to additions to the family and some dogs are better suited as companions than others. For example, some of the working breeds will 'work' other animals. Border collies are well known for rounding up cats, and terriers may just take exception to the pet gerbil.

Jem is also a herding dog and likes to use her 'eye' power; she will sit for hours on gerbil watch but she is not allowed to touch the cage.

Is This Your First Dog?

It is a simple question but so very important; and, almost as important, are you thinking of changing your regular breed? All dogs within a breed are different and all breeds are different, so if you are changing you will have the advantage of being an established dog owner but the disadvantage of having preconceived ideas of behaviour. If you are a first-time owner you will not have the advantage of being familiar with living with a dog, but your mind will be open to new ideas and breed characteristics. If you have never shared your life with a dog before you will have the first-time problems of when, where and which? We are all used to that feeling, whether it is when buying a car, a house, or looking for a new job; but this time you are dealing with another being and it will be dependent on you, so you need to get it as right as possible.

When to buy needs some forethought; what feels right for you may not be a good time for the rest of the family or for the availability of time. Make sure that you are able to give unconditionally of your time and patience and that you will not be torn between other commitments and people who are not dog compatible.

Where to find your dog is dependent on whether it is to be a puppy or a rescue, a pedigree or a cross-breed. If you have a particular breed in mind but want to give a home to a rescue you need to look for a rescue organization specializing in that breed. If you are giving a home to a rescue and have no preference as to breed then you need to visit non-specialist rescue organizations. Rescue centres have both older and younger dogs and puppies, but you may need to make several visits before you meet the dog for you. Never be tempted to take a dog because you feel sorry for it. You have to *want* the dog you are looking at and you have to *like* it. When a dog is in a state of neglect or despair it is easy to want to give it a home, but that same dog will be just as argumentative, cheeky and challenging as any other when it has regained its confidence. There may be times when your patience is stretched almost to the limit, so any reservations you may have had will suddenly return. You will love your dog or else you would not be taking him in, but you must also *like* everything about him, and the two are different. If you are looking for a puppy and one of a particular breed then you must pay attention to both the breeder and the family tree. Even at this stage it is wise to 'listen' to the dog's language, for the very appearance of the dogs and their attitude to the breeder will tell you what kind of a life they are leading and what the breeder is like with them. A dog should be pleased to see its owner, should not be nervous, nor should it be bad-mannered. Likewise, the puppies should be confident and happy in their surroundings, which should be clean and as near natural as possible. Both the parents (if the stud dog is not there make sure that he can be seen should you wish) should be in good condition and the puppies should look well cared for and well fed. If you are seeking a dog for a particular discipline or way of life ask about its ancestors and other progeny. Your puppy will have not just its parents' genes but those of many animals who went before it, and if other progeny has not made the grade then it may be that you need to be looking at other bloodlines.

Which breed of dog is, of course, your choice, but you still need to do some soul searching to make sure that your decision

Toy breeds, medium breeds and large breeds: within each of these you will find small, medium and large dogs. Certain characteristics are familiar to some breeds and small dogs may behave differently to large dogs, but do not allow a preconceived idea of small, medium and large to be the good, the bad and the ugly.

Aggression Often Arises from Uncertainty

It is not unusual for a small dog to be considered mild-mannered and a large dog to be presumed to be aggressive when quite often the reverse may be the case. Many people will make a detour around a large dog coming towards them but will actually approach a small one; granted that the smaller dog would be easier to deal with should it be unfriendly, but most people would not expect it to be anything other than friendly. The larger the dog, the more caution is shown, yet small or large, pure-bred or cross-bred, they are still dogs and will quite often be reflecting the handler or the type of handling they have been brought up with and the attitude of the person approaching them. If a small dog does not appear to pose a threat, the person approaching it will be more relaxed and therefore the dog will not pick up any fear or uncertainty. But if the person approaching a larger dog is apprehensive, the dog will sense this, feel intimidated and will put up an immediate defence, often causing a show of aggression but one which is originally born of apprehension.

If you have two dogs of different breeds it is sometimes better to match similar size and instincts, or make a compatible age gap. If these two dogs were to play energetically the larger one could unintentionally injure the smaller one. However, Bella is a small, mature dog and soon puts the young Hope in his place.

is right not only for you but also for the dog that is about to enter your life. For example, if you already have a dog and you would like to get a second one but one of a different breed then you would need to consider the compatibility of the two breeds and not just your desire to have the two of your choice.

Most people have a preference for a particular size of dog, and if you are a 'small-breed' person you may not have the

The Newfoundland Poppy is happy in the water following her working instinct.

Holly, on the right, is half Newfoundland and has the same instincts as kennel-mate Poppy.

Emma, peeping over the wall, is a collie and lives with Poppy and Holly. These three dogs are all strong working dogs, love water and can live together compatibly.

confidence to train a large-breed dog; similarly, if you prefer larger dogs you may not respect a smaller breed. Before you make your final decision you need to make sure that you have thought about all the long-term commitments and not just the first few weeks of your life together. You need to feel that you can both like and cope with the adult dog and not just with the growing version. The adult dog is the one you will be living with for a long time and the results of puppy-hood and how you deal with them will manifest themselves in the older dog, be it small, medium or large.

You need to be sensible in your approach to dog ownership. No matter how much love, care, exercise and mental stimulation you can possibly give, you will find it difficult to keep a St Bernard happy in a high-rise, one-room apartment; just as you would not purchase a Pekinese with the intention of doing working trials.

No matter what breed of dog you have in mind or how much love, time and attention you have to give, you will have to take into consideration your own living accommodation. There are no hard and fast rules as to which dog can live where, and, although there are many who would contradict this, it is not as important where the dog lives as to whom it is living with. Many dogs have perfect housing and are living in the kind of environment they are best suited to, yet they are not content or happy. Other dogs living in conditions some may condemn, for example, a small flat, may be perfectly content and have all they want, a partner who not only provides loving care but is also prepared to keep the dog mentally happy. Unfortunately, failing to keep a dog mentally happy may be a fault with many owners because they do not fully understand the dog's mental require-ments.

Dog ownership is common sense; if the motivation is right and the prospective owner is genuine, there needs only to be an understanding of which dog and how to understand it to keep it happy. Instead of expecting your dog to conform and live entirely by your rules, learn to see things from his point of view. Let's take a journey into his mind and see what he really thinks.

Chapter Summary

Understanding the natural instincts of a dog can make its training easier. When choosing a dog or puppy make sure that you choose a breed that is suitable for your lifestyle; and, if you already have a dog, make sure that your second one is of the same breed or of one that is compatible to the first.

CHAPTER 2

Who Is the Teacher?

How and when should we train? How should we learn to train? Dog training is considered to be an important part of dog ownership; it is often very basic and, rather like a jigsaw with some pieces missing, it can be confusing. The word which forms the missing link is 'understanding', and understanding the mind of a dog, seeing the world through its eyes rather than our own, is a slow but rewarding learning process.

We all have our own views on life and how we wish to spend each day, but simply by taking a dog into our homes we are preventing it from making its own choices. We can give it choices; it may be able to decide for itself whether to spend time in the garden or in the house. It may have a choice of which toy to play with, but the human being restricted it to the house and the garden and encouraged it to play with toys. In the wild it would be able to select its own grazing ground and would find something of its own choosing to play with. You may be assured that whatever it chose would not squeal, ring or rattle – all noises which a dog may relate to the stalking or killing of a small animal. If you are the pack leader, and you should be, it is certainly up to you to provide a safe pack area and to teach your pack how to live; but if you were a canine

To a human being a squeaky toy is a toy that squeaks, but part of a dog's natural instinct is to prey on small animals and they will squeak when caught. This is part of a young dog's education for learning how to survive and provide for itself. A squeaky toy to a dog can provoke a thought process that, if not correctly controlled, can lead to what to the dog is a natural progression of stalking and catching small prey, to chasing rabbits and eventually hens, birds or even sheep. Make sure your dog does not practise his survival skills on his toys!

SQUEAK!

A wild dog will practise its survival skills on small animals by stalking and killing them; this instinct is not needed in the domestic dog and so it must be harnessed. Attacking and shaking a squeaky toy can be related to the killing instinct and this dog has gone a stage further, it has followed its survival instinct by catching a mole. This can lead to larger problems later such as sheep chasing.

pack leader you would be providing things your dog could recognize. Recognition does not just come with seeing, it is part of a dog's genetic make-up, instincts going back for centuries are bred into them, telling them what is familiar and natural, and what is not. If you bend down and look at the world from your dog's height everything will seem quite different; you may stand up again

What you see is a nice, friendly horse.

What your dog sees; a huge monster, and if the horse were outside its legs would be frightening.

and recognize the world from your height but your dog will remain near to the floor. Just as there is a great difference in the way you both see the world, so is there a great difference in what you both expect from the world. Instincts vary according to the breed of dog, some are bred to work, some to retrieve, some to guard, but all have the same basic instinct to survive, and all recognize that there must be a pack leader, you or them. The smaller breeds are not as powerful and therefore their dominance is not easily recognizable, and the man-made breeds will not have the same instincts as the natural pack animals. Training is usually considered mainly in relation to the larger or original breeds, but the smallest of dog may benefit from living life as nature intended, as a dog.

So often we hear of 'dog ownership', the words almost seem to imply that you buy a dog, own it, and everything else fits into place. According to the dictionary to 'own' means to 'have as one's property, to possess'; but the concept of 'leadership' combined with control (to regulate or restrain) provides a more fitting description for the relationship between man and dog. You need an understanding, caring attitude with a willingness to adapt, finding out your dog's needs and requirements and tailoring both yours and his to find an acceptable accommodation.

There are several ways of learning how to train your dog. Your local library will have a selection of books on training and many bookshops will be able to give you a list of titles to choose from. Other dog handlers can be a mine of information, and if you look in your local papers you will probably find some dog-training and puppy classes which you might be able to attend.

The dog world can be rather like a minefield: there appear to be so many options and questions, how and where to train, what to feed, which toys, what kind of a bed. Each product claims to be the best and each well-meaning piece of advice you receive will probably be the correct way of training for the person who is trying to help you, but it may not necessarily be right for you or for your dog. Before you enter this territory and make a move you may later regret, stop and think for a while. Take a good look at your dog and at the kind of relationship you already have with it.

If you have little or no relationship with your dog then to attend a training class may not be the answer. If your dog has little or no respect for you as pack leader he will more than likely see the classes as an excuse for an hour of stupidity and play; this will not be beneficial for him and is not really fair on the other handlers. Rather than attend a class you would probably benefit more from tuition on a one-to-one basis; however, this may have pitfalls if you are not careful. You would need to know that the person to whom you are turning for guidance will be able not only to teach you but be able to give you what you *need* and not what they *think* you need. Often a specialist in the breed you have chosen will be better equipped to help you. But if your dog is quiet and shy and your newly found trainer is familiar only with the handling of arrogant or extrovert dogs, there is a possibility that the advice you receive may do more harm than good. It is always wise to find out as much as possible about any clubs or trainers and to attend as an observer before committing yourself and your dog to any classes or private tuition.

If you are looking for a book on training you will need something easy to understand which will teach you the fundamentals and not competition training. If you can find books specializing in your chosen breed then so much the better, for each breed comes with its own little foibles.

There are so many alternatives and each one may claim to be the answer, but let us go back to taking stock of this relationship and where you want it to go. Start thinking **dog**.

You have to learn to listen to your dog: it will let you know how it feels, what it needs, what is the best way to train it and whether it will be happy with the kind of life you have planned for it. If you have your heart set on competing in one of the many disciplines with your dog and, in the first few weeks of your being together it proves to be shy and introvert, it is telling you it may not be happy mixing with crowds of people and other dogs. You will have to 'read' your dog's actions to find out if it is naturally introvert or if, unwittingly, you have created a lack of confidence in its outlook on life. The former may mean that your dog will be happier with a quiet lifestyle and you may have to rethink your kind of life together (there are still many options available); the latter may just mean that spending time will give your dog the confidence he lacks. Even this kind of quality time needs careful consideration, for if he is not confident in *you* then socialization classes could make him worse; but, if he has been over-protected, then mixing with other dogs may be just what he needs. If you do not take the time to learn how to communicate with your dog then you will find it difficult to understand what he is trying to tell you and how you should answer him.

People are often patient in the initial stages of training, spending time teaching the dog the elements of good manners, and then, suddenly, they leap from teaching the elementary words (the basic commands) to a far more complicated language. Just as the dog is grasping the idea of 'sit' and 'heel' it is bombarded with full conversations – 'bring it here boy', 'fetch', 'where is it?' 'seek it out' – the list is endless and the dog will be ready to explode.

A golden rule of training is never ask the dog to do something that it is not yet ready to attempt. If it will not recall at five yards it certainly will not at ten. If it is not sitting when it is told, and first time, there is little point in trying to force more learning on to it. Time and patience are essential and if the training is done in a way the dog can relate to and at a speed it is comfortable with then the mistakes will be few and far between and will not be too difficult to correct.

If you feel that you need any form of help or training then you have a puppy or a new, older dog, or perhaps you are having problems with a dog you have had for a while. The simple fact that you need some training means that there is a breakdown in communication between you and your dog, and quite often what began as a slight problem becomes not only a bad habit but also a way of life for some dogs. If you now take this dog to someone else for training there is the danger of your dog respecting the trainer rather than you. If you go to classes and your dog behaves while he is there you may find that he will become condition-trained – behaving in the classes but still being bad-mannered at home.

Always try to simplify rather than to complicate, and try to look at your dog or

You and your dog can benefit when you attend a training class, but, just like a child going to school, your dog should learn the basics of good manners before being enrolled in order to avoid disrupting the class. If your dog is going to create a problem and you need help, ask the trainer about one-to-one tuition to begin with.

its problem from a different angle. For example, if you have a small child you try your best to make sure it has a certain amount of knowledge and manners *before* it goes to school. The same principle should apply to your dog. Do take part in training classes, do read books, but, no matter how hard it may seem to be, there is only one person who can make the relationship work and that is you. It is in your best interests to listen to all the advice you are given, but it is no good trying to take it all on board and trying to apply it all to you and your dog, for you are individuals and as such you need to sift through the information, discarding what you do not need.

How do you know what information to keep? It goes without saying that your dog should have good manners and this can only be achieved by gaining its respect and by its recognizing you as the pack leader, and, as in all forms of tuition, you need to communicate. Your dog is your best teacher; he will tell you what is going on in his mind, what he expects from you and how he intends to make sure you do his bidding, for, if you have provided him with an opportunity, he will endeavour to train you! Prevention is better than cure and if you are aware of your dog's thoughts you will also be aware of his intentions. When he is providing you with the information needed to train him, you will be ready and listening and will use it to your advantage and not his. With the best will in the world, no trainer can be a fly on your wall and no book can relate specifically to your dog.

Your dog is an individual and only by being close to him, watching his movements and his interactive response to your movements can you understand fully his requirements. You will spend many

Bess is determined to get her handler's attention. You will spend many hours in your dog's company so learn to 'listen' to his language for he will try hard to understand you and to communicate with you.

hours in your dog's company; if not, you should question why you have him, any dog large or small, companion or working companion, deserves friendship and communication. But do you make sense to him and do you listen to what he has to say to you? If you take the trouble to listen to him your dog will talk to you. You may not recognize his language to begin with, but then neither will he recognize yours.

As humans, we are all guilty of forgetting that our dogs do not come to us with a full knowledge of our language and ways of communication. It will benefit any dog handler to remember that their dog comes to them with a barren mind as regards our language. At no time does a dog knock on a door and ask to live with humans, learn their language and understand their culture. They could not care less, they have their own language, instincts and code of ethics and they are not interested in ours. If we wish to be able to communicate successfully we must find an acceptable medium. If we were to take up residence with another human being, from another country and speaking another language, we would take the time and make the effort to communicate with sign language, learn simple words and study each other's culture in order to be able to live in harmony. Yet we take a dog into our home for our own pleasure, spend a short time teaching some confusing sounds (for sounds are all words are to a dog) and before long we are expecting the poor dog to not only read our minds but be a super dog as well.

Even a rescue dog that may have suffered physical and verbal abuse can be taught a new language, one that he will not associate with his past. We would teach a dog that has suffered abuse that not all human contact means pain, we would need to be gentle. So we would find the kinds of sound that may upset the dog, drop those words from our 'dog vocabulary' and introduce a new language. For example, a rescue dog in my care was terrified every time he heard the word 'you'; realizing that this sound to him must have preceded some physical pain, I had to take care to make sure that the sound was omitted from his 'new' language. Bearing in mind that each word is a sound, this meant that such words as 'new' 'too' and 'shoo' could not be used either, for even with a different tone he was frightened. Eventually he gained confidence in me and I began to get him used to all sounds, including the ones he had been afraid of, not because I needed to use them but because it was possible that he might hear them elsewhere. In time he trusted me implicitly; he had learned a new language and any sounds (words) from his old language no longer concerned him, but it is impossible to guarantee that someone using the old sounds in a tone he recognized from his past would not upset him if I were not around to give him security. No matter how well you know your dog you cannot control its memory.

The only way to discover what upsets, agitates, excites or pleases your dog is to observe it; only by spending time watching and learning can you discover the secret of how to train your own dog. Although you will be training your dog and teaching it how to behave for you in your world, make no mistake about it – you have a lot to learn from your dog. Training is a learning process for both of you and you will learn to 'listen' to each other; the sooner you realize that your dog is capable of communicating with you on a regular basis the sooner you will find out how to gain access to his mind.

Chapter Summary

Learn to 'listen' to what your dog has to say. Keep the training simple and never introduce a new instruction until the present one has been understood. The gaining of your dog's respect is an important part of establishing yourself as pack leader.

CHAPTER 3

Training from the Cradle

Basic 'good-dog' behaviour should be part of everyday life; no one should accept bad manners in a dog as normal. Even with what may be initially classed as a 'problem' dog, with the correct attitude and training good manners should eventually become part of its life. Teaching a dog everyday commands, such as to sit or lie down, do not come into the category of good manners, they are a necessary part of the language you will teach your dog to enable it to understand certain requirements. Just as a parent will teach a small child a new word at every opportunity, so he or she will also have been making it quite clear to the child what is and what is not acceptable in the home. Good manners are for always and should become a way of life.

What Are Good Manners?

No one can decide for you your level of good manners. If you are happy for your dog to be on the furniture then it cannot be considered bad-mannered for your dog to be curled up on the settee when you enter the room; this is your dog and your rules are acceptable. However, if your dog sat on you, tried to push you off the settee or, even worse, tried to push someone else off, then there would be no excuse and this behaviour would be bad-mannered. If you do not allow your dog on the furniture

Texas is displaying good manners by waiting to be given permission to jump out of the car. He is standing in the doorway of a specially designed wire frame that forms two single compartments.

and it understands this rule and then you enter the room to find it occupying the most comfortable chair you know that it is being bad-mannered. If you are talking to someone and your dog is constantly pulling at the lead, whining and striving for your attention like a child, then it is displaying bad manners. If your dog pushes through doors in front of you, leaps in and out of the car with no regard for you and jumps up at or annoys other people then it is bad-mannered.

Manners are not negotiable: to become a valuable member of a pack a dog must learn how to behave, how to be acceptable to the elders and how to conduct itself in the pack life. If you are the pack leader then it is up to you to teach good manners, if not your dog will make the rules and it becomes a fine line between right and wrong. A dog that has been taught good manners is misbehaving when displaying bad manners; but a dog which has made its own rules is not misbehaving when it displays bad manners since it believes such behaviour to be correct. If you do not teach a set of rules then your dog cannot break them, it simply makes its own, and, while you are desperately trying to re-educate it, others will be subjected to its bad manners. For although in your house your rules apply, good manners must be in evidence for your dog to be both likeable and acceptable to other members of the family and the outside world.

There is a well-known story of a dog handler who, when replying to someone who commented on how lucky he was to have such a well-behaved dog, said, 'Luck has nothing to do with it, it was damned hard work.' The message is loud and clear: if you want your dog to be well-behaved you must be prepared to work at it. The harder you work, the easier your dog will be to train.

Puppy training should be looked on as creating a foundation. If the foundations for a building are of poor quality there will be problems with the building and restrictions to its size and usefulness. You would be unwise to try and build a large property on foundations that were of a quality barely good enough for a small bungalow. If you were to find that you needed to enlarge this property you would be advised to reinforce the foundations. If you lay a good foundation when training a puppy you will be making it easier to reach your dog's full potential, essential in competitive work and important for a happy home life. If you are working with an older dog, possibly a rescue, it is important to recognize that it may not have a solid training foundation, so be prepared to go right back to the beginning and start as if training a puppy. This is easier in that the older dog will have already developed a character for you to recognize, but harder due to the bad habits it will probably have picked up.

Puppy training is common sense, but unfortunately there is a trend to make it complicated. Conflicting advice can be gathered from different sources of information; this may cause confusion to new dog owners before they even begin training. 'Let a puppy enjoy its puppyhood'; 'Don't start training it until it is six months old and provide plenty of play and toys.' Such simple advice but it can cause so many problems. Would you really leave a toddler to enjoy its childhood with no guidelines to attempt to teach it manners and nothing but boxes full of toys to occupy it? I think not. The puppy advice is correct in the respect that it does need to enjoy its puppyhood, but this will be of a

If we throw a human being a ball they will catch it and associate it with play, if we throw them a bone they will not show any creative interest towards it. If we throw a dog a bone it will associate it with food and will know what to do with it. But if we throw a ball to a dog that has never seen one before it will not only not be interested in it but it could assume it was being thrown at it and not to it. This tells us that human toys are not a natural concept to a dog, and so for the first few weeks it is essential that your dog is introduced to recognizable things in its life to enable you to teach it acceptable manners within your pack.

better quality if it has sensible leadership and guidance; play and toys should be formative and serious competitive training should be delayed. A puppy is a young dog and as such it will need to be able to recognize certain actions and body language for it to be able to relate to its own instincts. Human beings are not canine and many of the human ideas of educating a young dog are more suited for a young child, for example, the toy box. We give children toys so that they can play and learn and in so doing the toys help to educate them; they can learn to count, read, write and draw all with the aid of toys; none of these skills applies to a dog. In the wild a puppy will play educational games, it will learn how to run,

swerve, turn sharply and it will interact with other puppies, finding great fun in chasing after them, and they will chew bones, these activities are hardly educational for a child.

Although we can compare the young dog and the young child during education, their instincts are entirely different. Centuries ago our instincts may have been similar to those of a pack dog; we lived and hunted in groups; we had 'pack' leaders; we were nomadic; we protected our own pack and looked after the environment by keeping our domestic area clean. Evolution has changed many of these instincts; as far as technology is concerned we have improved, but as regards the environment and our attitude

This is the canine way of introduction; it is not natural for dogs to shake hands as we do. The differences in the dog's instincts and ours signify the difference between the way we see the world and the way they see it.

to each other we could possibly learn some things from a thinking dog. Throughout our search to understand the mind of a dog, we can often make comparisons with groups with similar rules – a tribe of American Indians and their chief, an army and its general, employees and their employer. It is also helpful to look at some of the recognizable animal instincts in order to help to put things into perspective. For example, children play with toys; this is the human way of education, dogs sniff each other's tails, this is the canine way of introduction. What is recognizable to one is not even familiar to the other; if we are going to provide a dog with a human accessory we must make sure that it understands it as a dog.

There are varying patterns of behaviour in the many breeds of dog and training will always have to be adapted to

Puppies should never be denied human contact and interaction. There are some wonderful moments to be shared with a puppy, but if you cuddle one on the sofa when it is small do not blame it for sitting on the furniture when it is big. Olivia is having fun with these puppies while sitting on the ground.

suit the individual breed. For example, all puppies are lovable and cuddly; few people will be able to resist the temptation to sit and nurse the fluffy little bundle until it falls asleep. But if we look at this as from the dog's mind – if it can go to sleep on someone's knee while he or she is sitting on a chair, why should it be told off when it ventures on to the same chair without an invitation? Would it not be easier and clearer to the dog to sit and cuddle it on the floor, thus enjoying the chance to spend quality time with the youngster without confusing it? Always remember that puppies grow larger; it may be acceptable for a toy breed to spend time on the furniture when it is older, but a larger breed of dog can pose a problem. Even if you do not object to your big dog sharing your sofa, remember that the larger dog needs more exercise and is heavier than a toy breed; at some time it will probably come straight from a walk in the park and leap on to the furniture with wet paws. He is a dog, he does not understand human ways, why can he not go on the furniture when he chooses, wet paws or not?

It comes back to common sense: decide on your house rules at the beginning and educate your puppy or new dog to them as soon as possible. Do not be fooled into thinking that, because your little charge is a dog it cannot understand the rules, explain things carefully and thoroughly to your dog and you will be pleasantly surprised just how much it is capable of taking on board. The key word is 'explaining'; it is a common human fault to talk to the dog in human terms and expect it to understand and mind-read what we did not explain in full. It does not understand English or any other human language. If you take a baby and speak

Dogs do not understand our language; they learn certain words. A dog will learn 'sit' and 'stay' but if you bombard it with human language such as 'Wait a minute while I pop to the shop' the dog will sit and wonder what on earth you are on about. Here Dillon is clearly confused.

only one language to it, that is the only one it will understand; whatever words you teach your dog, that will be its language. It need not make sense to you: if you choose to say 'red paint' to make the dog sit down that will become part of its 'new' vocabulary. One young dog of mine used to work at full gallop and I taught her to go at a steadier pace to the word 'slow', this produced a nice, steady, loping pace from her. When she began to walk too fast and I said the word 'slow', she immediately began to go a little faster. To her the word 'slow' meant to go at a pace faster than a walk, a loping pace; common sense if you look at it from the dog's point of view.

Choose your 'dog language' carefully and make it uncomplicated. There is little point in telling your dog to 'Sit there a minute while I take my shopping from the car and put the kettle on.' Your keyword is 'sit', and in the training stages that is all your dog needs. Once again look at it from a different angle and think about a toddler just learning to speak: what would the next sentence mean to it? 'Hang on a minute while I pop to the shop and then I'll nip in the bath before we collapse with the telly.' Objectively considered, it is a strange way to speak, but I am sure that you can understand what the sentence means. It would all need to be simplified to the child who cannot yet speak or to someone not familiar with the English language. Teach your dog the key words and add your extra vocabulary at a later date when you have an understanding of each other.

It is never too late to train, but you must always start as you mean to go on. An older dog will soon accept the rules of a new home, even if its manners in its previous home left much to be desired. A dog allowed to make its own rules will soon begin to take both its home and leadership for granted and quite often we place the dog in hierarchy position without even realizing it. When a new puppy or an older dog comes into the home it will make mistakes and be bad-mannered in the first few days, and the humans involved will recognize these faults and determine to correct them when the dog is settled in. But this, of course, is not how the dog sees it, is it? It does not think, 'Yippee, I've got away with

this now but in a couple of weeks time they'll change the rules and I will have to behave.' No, he has entered the house, seen the rules, or lack of them, in the first few days, accepted things as he sees them and is quite happy about it. It will be a shock to his system if you change them again when your routine goes back to normal and you decide to 'sort him out'. But more than likely he will hang on to what he likes, home rule for Fido, and you will have a hard time correcting him.

It is all too common to leave a dog until it is five or even six months old before deciding to seek help in lead training and basic obedience; the thought being to allow the dog its playful youth. But, in fact, it has been allowed to believe that it has control of certain situations and you now have to convince it otherwise before you can expect success in training. A child will lead a happy and secure life if it is brought up to know both its mental and physical boundaries, how far away from parental control it may wander and how much Mum and Dad will allow before putting their foot down. A puppy needs to know the same boundaries. It is of little use allowing a puppy to run into a neighbour's garden to play with their children on Monday and then being annoyed with it for digging up the same garden on Tuesday. Physical boundaries. If you ask your young dog to sit down and it wanders around the kitchen and picks up a ball first, pushing you to keep repeating your command, you cannot expect it to sit down at the first request on any other occasion. Mental boundaries. Dogs are clever; they will put you in a position where you fall into the trap of repeating yourself and therefore give in to inconsistent training. If you wish your dog to respond to your first request you must

These two scenes may look the same but they are not. Your view is higher, focuses on the trees, and the ground gets only secondary attention.

Your dog's view focuses on the ground with the trees not even getting secondary attention because the scents of the earth, the sounds of moving insects and vibrations will take precedence. You are still interested in your walk but your dog's attention may already be diverted.

explain to it that this is what you expect. Notice the use of the word *request* and not *command*. A command to a child means do it now and with no negotiation; there is a subtle difference between, 'Please put your toys away' and 'Put your toys away now'. The first is a request and a well-behaved, well-mannered child will, nine times out of ten, respond, for if not parental displeasure may be shown. A wise parent can usually judge the response from the child before he speaks, thus making sure that the parent gets the desired response by requesting or commanding. Not everything is so clear-cut as this example, but if you always aim to do and give the best possible you will soon find it second nature to act on common sense. Transfer this same common sense to your dog: if you are willing to negotiate with him by repeating yourself, or by bribing him with food, you are proving to him that you are not capable of being in control or of being his pack leader. A dog with his attention on you and listening to your every word will

'recall' at a request tone of voice, but a dog distracted and not concentrating on you will need a command tone for a 'recall' to ensure that there is no negotiation. Someone has to be leader and if it is not you it will be him, from the smallest of the toy breeds to the largest hunting or working dog someone has to be in charge. The only difference between the small breeds and the larger ones is the degree of strength and the determination to lead. Most of the toy breeds are perfectly happy doing things which would not be acceptable in a larger breed. A small dog pulling on a lead is usually not in danger of pulling anyone over; but even a small dog can cause damage if it bites or chews. Any dog allowed a plentiful supply of toys at any one time will be induced into excited play and will be tempted to chew or destroy some of its possessions. If you allow this, why can it not do the same to your possessions? Common sense again, and the only way to take control is by teaching from the cradle. Allow your puppy to be a puppy, but one with good manners.

Chapter Summary

Good manners should become a way of life. Use common sense in all training, decide on your house rules at the beginning and educate your puppy or new dog to them as soon as possible. Do not allow your dog to manipulate you into the repetition of your commands.

CHAPTER 4

Your Dog's Thoughts

Does a dog think? To train your dog you are beginning to learn how to 'think dog', but does your dog think or, more to the point, do you want it to? Never fall into the trap of making things more complicated than they are, always try to make things more simple. Of course, a dog thinks; I am one of those stubborn people who will defy all scientific explanations and argue with anyone who says a dog does not think. Dogs may not have the same kinds of thought as human beings, but they cannot exist without a thought process and they have the ability to work certain situations out for themselves if they are allowed to do so and they also have excellent memories. On more than one occasion I have taken my dogs to a competition and the following year they have repeated certain actions from the previous year.

Thinking is part of education; mental stimulation is the process of educating the mind and stretching it in order for it to take on board more information. In the wild a dog's thought processes will for most of the time be connected with survival, but that activity can cover a variety of different thoughts. What to eat and where to find it, finding a mate, protecting a mate or pack, the pack or pecking order, teaching the young, learning from the elders, it is all instinctive, but it must still be worked out.

If a child is not educated, taught manners or civilized it will not be able to read or write, work a computer or hold a conversation, but it will still be able to think; its thoughts will just be limited to its immediate surroundings and survival. But if a child is fed information its capabilities for working out situations will be far greater; it will see further than its immediate surroundings and it will begin to have a thirst for more knowledge. If the child is given the education with care and forethought it will grow into a responsible adult, but if its education is not sufficient to give it a sense of its mental and physical boundaries and the difference between right and wrong there is a danger that it will grow into an undesirable adult. Mental and physical boundaries are unwritten laws for all species, for without them there is no order to the group, be it a pack, pride, clan, tribe or family.

I believe strongly in going back to the basics if I am looking for an answer: if a building has a flaw then the foundations must be checked, if a dog has a problem go back to basics. Basic training is teaching a dog how to control its instincts and in some cases to rechannel them.

House training is a good example, for a well-educated dog will not wish to foul its bed; but it will see no reason why it cannot foul outside its own area and, if that happens to be your front room, then so be it. It is up to the human being to

We must always take into consideration not just what our dogs are thinking but what other animals think about them. It is a mistake to think that because your dog is not interested in another animal it will not create a reaction. This dog may not be interested in sheep, but when the sleepy ewe becomes aware of the dog she will run in fright, this will start the flock running and may even tempt the dog to give chase. If the sheep are in lamb they could suffer serious harm.

explain just how much of the area is to be kept clean and to teach where fouling is acceptable – rechannelling the canine instinct to fit in with the human require-ments.

Before the basic training comes the basic instinct, and the basic instinct of a dog is no different from that of a human, to survive. Human beings have come a long way from the days of the caveman and with this advance they have stretched their thoughts, introduced new ones and educated themselves to keep taking on board new information. When you take a dog into your home you are immediately stretching its natural, instinctive thoughts: you tell it where it can sleep, where it is allowed to go and where it must not go. It would learn similar rules in the pack, but they would

be easy to understand for it would be able to follow examples and would understand the language of its elders. Because we do not behave like dogs we must take every care to communicate in a dog language so as to make it both easier and quicker for the new dog to understand our rules. So with constant communication you are already stretching your dog's mind. You are giving it information and it will soon be asking for more.

How Intelligent Is Your Dog?

I would be rich if I had a pound for every time I hear people practically apologize for their dog's intelligence level. Either the dog is 'only a –' (whatever breed it may be but is considered not quite bright enough) or 'My dog is too intelligent, it is always trying to outwit me.' Not all dogs have the same level of intelligence and not all dogs have the same capabilities of working things out; their breed dictates only their instincts, what we do with those instincts is up to us and it is quite a responsibility.

Let us go back to humans for a moment. If we take two children, one genetically academic and one genetically less academic and we starve the first of any mental stimulation or information and feed the second with as much mental stimulation as possible. The second will be of a good inquiring mind and the first will be reliant on instinct only.

If someone has a dog of a known working breed, for example a Border Collie, a German Shepherd, a Husky or a Springer Spaniel, and does not feed its mind it will more than likely make up its own games which will probably be at the owner's expense, whereas a breed of dog recognized for being more docile would probably be quite content to chew a few toys and then go to sleep. Knowing this, people are usually very conscious that they must get the former kind of dog only if they have the time to devote to it in order to keep it out of mischief and the latter kind often goes to a home where it receives little mental stimulation. Yet surely we owe it to our dogs to stretch their minds in order for them to be able to communicate with us and for them to reach their full potential. We must, however, be guided by their natural instincts: a working breed will have instincts according to its breeding, for example a gun dog will be a fast dog and inclined to retrieve, a sheepdog will be a natural herder, and these traits must be remembered when training.

A Little Knowledge Can Lead to Mischief

If we take a docile breed and we do not stimulate its mind we could almost be guilty of keeping the dog docile for our own convenience. If we take a quicker-minded dog and over stimulate it we could be guilty of giving it a little knowledge and then allowing it to draw its own conclusions. For example, the first kind of dog can be given a toy, taught a game and then left on its own. It will play for a while, it may chew the toy, it may even chew something else, but its mind will not be inquiring and it will eventually settle down. The second kind of dog, given a toy and taught a game and then left on its own will devise all sorts of weird and wonderful things to do with the toy. It will make a thud if thrown against the door and a lovely, repetitive banging if rolled downstairs, it will make a wonderful mess if it is chewed along with the feather cushions – and let's eat the best shoes while we are at it! This dog was given stimulation that humans understand and not taught how to respect the pack nor how to be content with its own company; but the first dog had not been encouraged to think at all other than as a basic human game.

A child kept in isolation with no mental stimulation and no physical or verbal contact may reach a physical age of ten with the mental attitude of a baby. A dog given the same repetitive behaviour pattern day after day will remain at that level of stimulation; to stretch its mind and encourage it to develop mentally you must keep updating the information you give it.

Floss is a well-mannered dog and she knows she must not touch human food. We can almost imagine what she is saying, 'I am ignoring this sandwich, in fact it doesn't exist.'

'Well, maybe it does and one little sniff won't hurt will it?'

Do You Really Want Your Dog to Think?

Of course you do, why else would you have a dog if you did not want it to reach its full potential both physically and mentally? But because human beings and dogs are different species with different instincts, we often fall short on understanding or recognizing the dog's thoughts and where they are taking it. A dog understands things that are familiar to its instincts, it knows instinctively what to do with a bone but it has no natural reaction to a squeaky toy. If a human being provides a squeaky toy the dog will be shown a game to play and it will then relate it to an instinct, so the toy could be seen as a small, squeaky, odourless animal to attack. If the human being encourages or allows the dog to use its

'Oops, better not, I don't like mustard anyway!'

teeth on the toy the dog may then believe it is right to destroy it. If the toy is used to make the dog think of other instincts it will use its mind in a more constructive way and will not feel the need to destroy. A dog will track its prey, it will search for it and stalk it, it will also play for hours a game which appears to a human being like 'tag' but is the pack's way of learning the twisting and turning techniques needed for hunting. The survival game is a game of interaction all puppies will play whatever their breed. All these instincts can be channelled into constructive, educational games, hide the ball, find the ball, stalk the ball, play a game of dodge the ball. Any game you play with your dog should be a part of education, and in order for your dog to learn it has to keep its 'sensible head' on. If someone is trying to teach their dog to 'find the ball' and keeps encouraging it with excited tones and wild arm gestures (erratic body language to a dog) it will find it difficult to pick up the message they are trying to relay. It will also become so excited it will forget what it is supposed to be doing and will jump around barking and yapping. When it does eventually find the ball, and probably with a great deal of human intervention, it will be on a note of hysteria and may not even remember how it came to do so; it will also be so wound up that it will be unable to settle down and if left alone will look for mischief. If the game were to be done by quietly encouraging the dog to use its brain and to work out where the ball is, and what to do with it once found, the dog will be stretching its powers of deduction. It will also be receiving mental stimulation and afterwards will be content to rest and be happy with its own company. Of course, the game may not have proved to be madly exciting for the

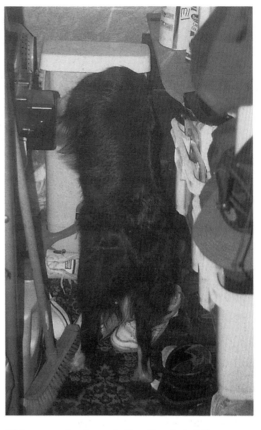

If dogs are kept mentally stimulated they learn to work things out; they can watch and wait and then set off on a mission. Floss knows that her food is kept in a bin in the utility room so she sees nothing wrong in opening the door, lifting the lid and helping herself. But she is not a thief!

owner, but the aim is to stimulate, exercise and educate the dog, which means teaching it in a way it understands and can appreciate – and not many dogs understand aerobics. Human beings play some games which really have no useful place in survival – throwing and catching a ball are not stimulating our brain, they are merely making us better co-ordinated at catching; but as the game is simple it is not difficult and can also become boring. Yet we insist that a dog play this game until it is overexcited and acting in neither a dog nor a human way. If the dog is used to mental stimulation it will become bored and devise a new game; if it is not used to thinking it will continue to 'retrieve' without any stimulation other than the physical, which can make it stiff and sore and could even lead to damage.

How Good Is a Dog's Memory?

Most people who share their lives with a dog will have been amazed at its ability to remember certain things; in fact, dogs may have a greater accumulation of 'memory information' than we often give them credit for. Although we can all appreciate that dogs do not sit down of a night reminiscing about their youth and that date to end all dates, they do keep information stored and they can both surprise and embarrass us with it. They can even act quite out of character when their memories are jogged. I am going to give some case histories now, for I believe that to understand the dog's ability to remember certain things can help in his training.

Meg. I have always been involved in sheepdog trialling and when Meg was four years old we competed at a large hill trial. It was a huge course and the sheep were on top of the hill and barely visible, so, as Meg made her way up the course, I whistled her to run out much wider. The following year I attended the same trial and arrived on the course just as my name was called to run. There was no time for my dog to 'study form' yet she ran

wider, as if commanded, at the exact same place where I had whistled her the previous year.

Skye. Five years old and running in a competition she finished her run and sat by the car drinking while I chatted to a friend, who just happened to lean a sack of dog food against my car. Five minutes after this we were working at the top of the field. The following week she competed and sat by the car again; another friend just happened to lean a sack of food against the car as we talked. Five minutes later and my dog had gone to work without me, unfortunately she did not realize that we were not on duty that day.

Laddie. Rescued at eighteen months old after having suffered severe beatings, it took months of patience to gain his trust. But for many years the sight of a man with a beard or wearing a deerstalker hat produced deep growling, and the smell of carbolic was enough to make him attack the nearest person. Only gaining his confidence and giving him time resolved these problems, but, even when he appeared to have no fear, I was always cautious, for we can never know what another person may smell of or do to rekindle a memory.

These dogs all displayed the ability to remember events and situations. Meg remembered the course and on her run she expected the same command she had received before and acted accordingly, even after a year. Skye remembered the situation and, because she wanted to work, it suited her to act on the memory. Laddie remembered pain; certain smells and a certain type of person rekindled something which caused reactions. In these three cases I knew what the memory was and could act accordingly, but the following has to this day kept me guessing. My daughter and I were giving a talk at a local school and decided to give the students a dog and duck demonstration afterwards. This involved six children standing in a line while the dog weaved the ducks in-between them. As I supplied a commentary, my daughter worked my wonderful old dog Moss. He was the most perfect gentleman anyone could ever wish to meet, he never showed aggression to any living thing and was wonderful with both mentally and physically handicapped children. Moss performed his duty with eagerness until he drew level with one of the girls when he immediately pulled away; my daughter guided him through the rest of the demonstration making sure that he did not work near this student. Afterwards we mentioned it to members of staff and were told that the child did not mix, had no friends and was unsociable but they could not give a reason why. Whatever it was, Moss had detected something and for the only time in his life he showed dislike of a human being.

These accounts provide valuable information for us; we can see that a dog can remember certain things and situations, it is able to relate certain sights or smells to something which can please or frighten it and can sense something that we humans may not even be aware of. Yet how often do we disregard the natural 'conversation' of a dog and insist that it does something against its wishes. It may be because we have not thought it out or, selfishly, it may not suit us to recognize what the animal is telling us. For example, the dog that does not like the next-door neighbour will have its own reasons; it may not know the neighbour well enough or possibly he stirs an

unpleasant memory or has done something to offend the dog without even realizing it. Whatever the reason, trying to persuade the dog to like this person may result in an obstinate front, whereas left to time, patience and some clever manipulation things could be different. A chance meeting on neutral ground with no eye contact and no threat of physical contact and the dog may come to see the person as no threat. But if the dog really does not like this person then so be it; we would obviously not force a human member of our family into a contact that made him or her uncomfortable.

Do We React Differently to Breed and Size?

Physical appearances govern our reactions in many instances and not just in relating to dogs. I remember long ago that when I took my driving test I had to wait for almost twenty minutes for the examiner to arrive and I watched all the other nervous learner drivers going to their cars with sympathetic-looking examiners. When a voice boomed my name and was followed by the appearance of the largest man I had ever seen and one who could hardly fit into my small car I was shattered. What chance had I of passing the test with such a monster? Yet he was the sweetest, kindest man I could ever have wished to meet and I did pass the test, but it took some time for my nerves to settle I may say.

Those sweet, little dogs that look as though butter would not melt in their mouths may be just as angry as a larger dog, and they have same kinds of like and dislike. They are just easier to pick up, lighter to deal with and often appear

Little, fluffy dogs are often not seen as a threat, but many of them are quite capable of trying to rule the world. This little chap is lovable and is not aggressive, but if he were he would not be considered as dangerous as a big dog, yet his teeth could still do serious harm to a child. All dogs should be respected but not automatically judged by their size.

Big dogs are often assumed to be aggressive, and yet many are just sweet, gentle giants. But if passers-by react apprehensively to big dogs they may induce fear or aggression in the dog without realizing it.

unnoticed if they are quiet. But those huge monster dogs with large eyes and even larger teeth are spotted immediately and are often judged to be guilty without an offence having been committed. Yet so many are like my driving examiner: they just need a chance to be seen as a living being with a right to its own space. It would make sense to treat any dog that may constitute a threat with caution, but then no dog should be a threat if it is on a lead and strangers do not invade its space. You can live with a dog for all of its life and not know its every thought, so it would be impossible to know what a strange dog's reaction would be. Just as we treat unfamiliar human beings with caution and respect, so should we treat dogs; after all, we do not approach strangers in the street and hug them, neither do we stare at them and pat them as we walk past.

Thoughts on Boarding Kennels

Some dogs may never see the inside of a boarding kennel, but for some it is almost a way of life. Some owners feel so guilty at leaving their dog that they are unhappy

Dogs booked into this boarding kennels have outside runs in a private garden. A clean yard surrounded by trees and flowers is usually a good guide to a well-run establishment.

for the duration of the separation and others entrust their dog to the kennel owner and spare them not a thought until it is time to take them home again. We are all individuals and what works for one person may not be right for another, but finally it is really about what is best for the dog. Dogs are put into kennels for a variety of reasons; the family may be holidaying where dogs cannot go; there may be an illness or a work commitment. Whatever the reason, the dog may be better in good kennels rather than being subjected to a variety of dog sitters or a strange home with the added risk of his running away and getting lost or run over. However, if a dog can be left in familiar surroundings with someone it both knows and trusts and someone that you trust with your dog then it would be the obvious choice, but not everyone has that reliable someone to fall back on. Many dog owners holiday in dog-friendly resorts and countryside either camping,

self-catering or in accommodation that accepts dogs. But we are all individuals and the same kind of holiday does not appeal to everyone.

So what does the dog think about this temporary accommodation? To begin with we have to see it from the dog's point of view, how it thinks as a dog and not how we think it should react. It has no idea when it goes into kennels that the owner will be coming back for it, but if it is a well-adjusted dog, trusts its owner and they share a good relationship, then it should go into the kennels and be confident that life will still be good. But if it has no respect for its owner it will probably see the kennels as a new challenge and be quite happy to try to add it and its inhabitants to its list of conquests. A timid, nervous dog may suffer in kennels, particularly if the owner is not sympathetic to its needs; but if a dog is not going to settle then it is not advisable to put it into kennels. Irreparable damage can be done to the relationship of dog and owner if the partnership is subjected to a shattering of confidence before the dog has gained complete trust.

Although a dog does not know what is happening the first time it goes into a kennels, it can soon settle down if it is handled correctly and it has something familiar with it. So the first essential is to make sure that the kennels is a good one; if there is any doubt at all then it should not be considered and cost should not be a key factor, for, although there is no need to pay exorbitant fees, it is not in the dog's best interests to cut corners. It is worth booking a dog in for two or three nights several weeks before the main event so that it can be used to the idea and become familiar with the kennel routine. Leaving a toy is not always the best idea as it will expect someone to play with it and may feel neglected if it does not happen. Far better a familiar rug or a friendly-smelling sweater for it to associate with home. I do not run a boarding kennels but dogs do occasionally stay with me for training, they arrive with coats, jumpers and sweaters for comfort but within a couple of days they have settled in with no whining or refusing to eat. If they have a ball or a toy they quite often annoy the other dogs and become quite offended when their demands to play are not met. However, I spend a lot of time in sight of them but I never force my attentions on them and as a result they soon trust me, feel confident and lose any insecurities they may have felt. When their owners pick them up they go ecstatic and jump all over them making it appear as if they have been sitting every day just waiting for their return, when in actual fact they were quite happy. It takes a long time for a dog to settle to a 'new' pack and the stay

The inside of the kennels should be as tidy as the outside. These are clean and light; each dog has its own pen with an outside run and they are never left unattended.

in kennels is not long enough for that, but if the dog recognizes certain pack behaviour, which a good kennel owner should instinctively feel, then it will feel more at ease.

Studying their behaviour, I would say that when the dog is made to feel secure it soon settles down and, if its 'new' life agrees with it, then in nine out of ten cases it will begin to adjust. As it settles down and becomes more secure it no longer needs the security of the familiar 'bed' it came in with, but when it sees its owners the thoughts of pleasure are immediately triggered off and it is overjoyed to be with them. However, not all dogs will settle, for not all kennels can cater for them in the same way; they are commercial enterprises so there will be many dogs of several breeds and there may be more than one dog walker attending to them. If the kennels has a routine then the dog will have to abide by it regardless of whether it makes it happy or not, so a smaller, family-run kennels would appear to be the more obvious choice.

The dog owners' behaviour is important for they will be packing cases and will more than likely spend more time with the dog whenever possible; thus the dog will soon suspect that something is amiss and begin to feel insecure. Just as with a child in a thunderstorm, it is far better to behave as normally as possible, and a tearful farewell at the kennels gate is not what the dog needs; instead the owner must make the dog feel that all is well and it is just a slight change in routine.

Travelling in Cars

A car is completely alien to dogs and the feeling of movement must be very disconcerting for them when they are not used

Dogs are safer if they cannot jump out of cars, and if they are in a cage they cannot distract the driver. Estate cars can be fitted with special wire grids to keep dogs secure when they are travelling. Rocky, Fudge and Twix share one large compartment.

Gemma and Floss are sharing a compartment that is shaped to fit the sloping back of the estate car.

to it. If a puppy is introduced to a car at an early age it will soon become used to the motion and will take it for granted. Unfortunately, we humans tend to expect dogs to react in a similar way to us and we tend to think that they appreciate the same things we do. But do they? Dogs can feel secure when they are in a small space and quite often if they are in a box, crate, or small, safe bed in a car they will learn to be content. It is even better if the dog's bed or sleeping blanket can be used in the car for it will trigger off the thought of sleep or of settling down and the dog will feel more secure. But if it is on a seat or sits in the back of an estate car what does

it see? Cars, buses, lorries and, of course, those loud motorcycles all rushing past making noise. When there are no wheeled monsters to watch, the very scenery it is used to living in is suddenly rushing past at great speed making the poor four-legged, first-time traveller feel quite disoriented, for there is nothing in its instinct to compare with this. We may enjoy the scenery but does the dog?

By now we have learned a little more about the dog's thought processes and its way of reasoning and so we know that the dog will remember some things from its past when certain situations trigger off the memory. If its first car journey is traumatic its memory will tell it to be alarmed every time it thinks it is going in a car. Every care must be taken to make sure the dog feels secure, trusts its human family and is neither threatened nor frightened by its first car journey. When travelling with a dog in a car I believe there to be only one thing more distressing than an unhappy dog and that is one that firmly believes it has the right to challenge every moving thing on the outside of the car. This dog will be jumping around, barking and making a general nuisance of itself when most children would be severely told off for similar behaviour, and this behaviour in the dog is usually a result of its being encouraged to chase and catch things moving at great speed. This is a case of a human game and animal instinct at cross-purposes. The human chases for fun but the dog would instinctively learn this behaviour for hunting and, if misinterpreted by the dog, it can confuse the survival instinct, which is serious, with the play instinct which results in the dog's not 'thinking' when it sees movement.

By now we are beginning to see a little into the dog's mind, the way it thinks, how it reasons and how it sees our world, now it is time to learn how to communicate with him.

Chapter Summary

Dogs can often associate certain actions or smells with memories that may be either pleasant or unpleasant, this can often make them to appear to be acting out of character. It is important that a new experience, such as travelling in a car or being in boarding kennels, carries only pleasant memories.

CHAPTER 5

The Silent Word

To enable the handler and the dog to communicate they need to find a common language, one they can both understand. We may not be able to 'talk dog language' but we are able to understand our dog's simplest requests. Think about your dog and take the time to study the way he tries to communicate with you; how do you know when he is hungry, thirsty, needs to go out? Your actions and *voice* can tell your dog when you are eating, walking, happy, sad, playing, angry; he has no voice to compare with yours, however, his eyes, ears, tail and the set of his body, in fact, his every movement will tell you something if you take the time to learn.

To begin with the language appears

Understanding basic dog 'language' is not difficult; for example, Monty is panting while he is not using energy, therefore he may be asking for a drink. Body language resembles the key words in our language, we use it as a foundation to build a larger vocabulary on.

easy. If your dog wags his tail he is happy, if he drops his tail he is sad, if he goes to his feed bowl he is hungry and a dog panting may be ready for a drink. Your language is just as easy: if you pick up his dish then food is imminent, if you pick up the lead or put on certain items of clothing you could be going for a walk. A smile on your face means you are pleased and if you look stern you are angry. At this point both dog and handler are communicating in the simplest form, but each one is putting his own interpretation on the body language.

Tail Wagging

When your dog wags his tail you may assume that he is happy, but his body movements interacting with his tail may tell a different story. If a dog is stiff-legged, head erect, with a small move-ment of the tail, which is held high, the chances are that he is facing another dog and may even be thinking of showing arrogance. A bitch greeting her puppies will have a totally different tail wag to the one she greets her handler with, and a dog barking and yapping with its tail wagging could be verging on hysteria.

Lowered Tail

A dog is not always unhappy when its tail carriage is low; it may be showing subservience to another dog (this does not necessarily mean unhappiness; just acceptance of the pecking order). Some dogs have a naturally low tail carriage and many dogs that are thinking or working carry their tails low. Almost like a gear lever, the tail has its positions and

the fear position on a normally long-tailed dog is almost underneath it. Not all dogs have the same kind of tail carriage, some are held naturally high, some do not 'hang straight' and some have no tail at all. But this does not mean that these dogs have difficulty in communicating, for they all have natural body movements and a language that is familiar to their breed, and each one will be able to 'talk' to an understanding handler.

Dogs have a way of working things out for themselves. A distressed handler may not be annoyed with their dog; they could just be having a bad day. If the dog under-stands the 'language' of that human it will know where the anger is directed and will soon know whether to apologize for a wrongdoing or just keep out of the way until the day improves. When the rela-tionship between dog and human has reached the stage where each can have a bad-mood day without the other's taking offence, then they are beginning to have empathy with each other and the human will find him- or herself automatically 'thinking dog'. It is worth bearing in mind that it is far easier and quicker for us to 'think dog' than it is for a dog to 'think human'. We know we need to communi-cate and understand the dog, but the dog is not initially bothered about under-standing humans.

You need to be able to understand what your dog is 'saying' to you to be able to correct him if he is about to step out of line. Prevention is better than cure and most dogs will 'tell' you what they are going to do seconds before they do it. For instance, let us look at the dog who only 'stays' for a few seconds before giving himself permission to move. This dog will know you are watching him and will test your ability to read him: a slight drop of the shoulder or twitch of the haunches and he is saying, 'I'm off, stop me if you can!' The dog showing aggression to other dogs will let you know by the look in his eye which dog he is going to pick on and when. If you spend time observing your dog's behaviour you will soon learn to understand his language, but if you then choose to ignore his statements you run the risk of having a bad-mannered dog.

Imagine a child in the company of adults: wise parents will observe their offspring carefully and at the first sign that junior's manners may be forgotten they will give a small warning nudge or a look. This discreet warning will usually be enough to prevent the child from over-stepping the permitted boundaries and then the cure does not become necessary. I can distinctly remember complimenting my children on their good behaviour whenever they were in the company of strangers; I felt that, although they could test my patience at home (as children have a habit of doing), they were never guilty of showing me up when in public. Their reply was, 'We couldn't, whenever we thought about it you gave us "the look"'. A look which, I have to say, I not only failed miserably to produce when they reached adulthood but have been warned that I am in danger of being on the receiving end of as I reach my (according to them) more senile years. I take heart that I taught my offspring how to be strong pack leaders when they left my regime and began their own.

If you are in tune with your dog's thoughts and understand his language then you will soon learn to read his inten-tions, almost before he knows himself what he is about to do, and with this fore-warning you can prevent him from over-stepping the boundaries of good manners.

Remember that your dog is to be part of your pack and, unlike children, you are not grooming him to be a future pack leader; he must realize that there is only ever going to be one leader and that is you.

Dogs 'Talk' to Each Other

Dogs do not have a problem in under-standing each other; dogs of the same breed understand their own 'accents' and dogs of different breeds understand the universal 'dog body language'. If we find it difficult to understand them it is because we do not observe all their movements as a language; we see it as actions and not always actions with intentions. If we were in a room full of people speaking different languages, and none that we understood, we would automatically watch every move they made so as to enable us to be able to interpret what they were saying, and, we would hope, be able to keep up with the conversation. Just by observing their body language we would know who was relaxed, who was tense, who was arguing and who was deep in thought. When two dogs approach each other they will immediately react, messages can come from the position of the tail, is it high or low, stiff or wagging? The head carriage, is it high and arrogant, low and aggressive, turning and nervous? The hair on the dog's back and neck, is it flat or is it beginning to rise up? The legs, are they taking a firm stance or are they preparing to back off? All these body movements will forewarn you of your dog's intentions to the other dog, and as yet there has not been a sound. If the dog does make a sound it will correspond with the body language; if the dog is friendly

Dogs talk to each other. These are finding out about one another and are introducing themselves. Note the tail positions, they are not yet relaxed in each other's company and their body language reflects this.

the tone will be light and friendly. If the dog is nervous, the tone will be either a nervous whimper or a light growl of nervous aggression. If the dog is aggressive the tone will be a deep-throated growl. Body language, growls and barks will all differ according to the size and breed of the dog, just as we all have different accents and languages. But in the same way we can tell by another person's tone or body movement what his intentions are likely to be. Similarly, all dogs have a universal language that is recognizable by other dogs, and by humans if they take the time to observe closely.

These dogs are having a social gathering with the older dog keeping order. Here she is 'talking' to a younger dog.

The younger dog is raising a paw to play; this is clearly an invasion of space to the older dog and she is telling him so. Note that the dogs in the background are keeping a wary eye on the proceedings and are not intruding on the space of the other two, but their body language is alert.

Dogs will 'converse' by body language when they first see each other; they will recognize certain movements and act accordingly. If one dog is showing apprehension the other may approach with a slightly aggressive attitude, warning the first dog that it feels superior. If the first dog retaliates then the second one will have to make the decision to become aggressive or to back down; but if the first dog does not retaliate then dog number two does not necessarily have to show any stronger show of aggression, but it will hold a dominant stance for a little longer just to make sure its intentions are understood.

When dogs are living in the wild they will not make a decision to fight for the fun of it, they are far too busy being self-sufficient, but if they or their pack are

The younger dog has deemed it wiser to bow to seniority and any possible incident has been diverted through this submission. The dogs in the background are considering interfering.

Introduction is nearly over and the older dog has made her point; as there is no sign of aggression the other dogs have decided to mind their own business and junior will soon be able to join them.

if this space is threatened it will act accordingly. Some dogs lose some of their protective instinct towards this space when they are living in a human environment, but it can still usually be seen in certain circumstances, for example, when they meet another dog, when they are eating or when they are digging. If a dog sees itself as pack leader and it is not a natural leader it will protect its space with nervous aggression. If a dog is a natural pack leader and it assumes this role over a human being its protection of its space may be threateningly aggressive. This can become a serious problem with larger dogs or of dogs of a dominant breed.

With good management and the assuming of the role of pack leader by the handler, the dog's space is not a problem. If the dog trusts its handler it will know that he or she would not let anything harmful or threatening into its space and a good handler will be protective of it. It is essential that the dog's right to this space is respected also, and so is knowing just how large this distance is. For example, some dogs may be on the alert when a 'threat' is ten yards away, some hardly notice the 'threat', and some may show signs of awareness when the 'threat' is twenty to thirty yards away. Anything can trigger a dog's awareness: it may be another dog, an approaching stranger, a car, or even something that the dog's owner does not see as being a problem; if the dog thinks it is a problem then it also thinks it has a reason to be protective. We can now see a good reason for making sure that we assume leadership, for the role of a good pack leader is to protect and offer security. We can also deduce from this information that, if the dog is in front of the handler, in the leadership position,

under threat then they will become aggressive. They will also make sure they observe the rule of 'space' and this is one golden rule that is often left unattended to in the domestic human–dog pack. In the wild dogs can create their own space; in the domestic dog world they are often forced to have their space invaded.

A Dog's Natural Space

Each dog will instinctively have its own 'space'. This is the area surrounding it that it considers to be its safety area, and it is also nearer to the 'threat'; but if the handler moves between the dog and the 'threat' he or she takes control of how to deal with it. The handler's body language will tell the dog what to expect, for if the handler is fussing over the dog or is bending down the dog will not feel as protected as if the handler took a strong upright stance and was determined in guarding the 'pack'.

Is Our Body Language 'Natural'?

We do have a natural, animal body language, but it is usually deep within us and even if we sense it we are often afraid to use it. Our gut reactions usually reflect our natural instincts, but we so often do not have the courage to use them or we are indecisive. How often do we say after the event, 'I thought it was wrong at the time but I didn't like to say so'? That same instinct, if we listen to it, will allow us to become a 'natural' leader, for it will tell us how to use our body language. Quite often people find that their dog will come back to them when they turn and walk away; a dog expects the pack leader to go when he is ready and the pack must follow. But we then make it into a game and do not follow through with what our dogs expect. But if we used this method from the very first meeting with our new charge, be it young or old, it would have something to recognize.

We use hand movements to point to the floor to encourage a dog to lie down, make a dog stay and to keep it to our side, but a dog does not instantly recognize these movements, they are not natural to it. So we are, in fact, teaching two languages. The first one is our vocal language and

the second one is the body language we want the dog to understand. But what about the body language the dog naturally understands, the one that will make communication quicker and easier between handler and dog? To begin with, we must appear to know what we are doing and this means a posture the dog will recognize. If we are stooped and appear indecisive the dog will not see a strong leader; if we are stiff and stand with our legs ready for making a strong stance we will appear aggressive. But if we are tall, gentle, strong and fluid in our movements the dog will instinctively recognize a familiar body language, and one to be associated with someone of leader material.

The Importance of Suppleness

Naturally your dog needs to be supple, and it will be, for by interacting with puppies in a litter and with its mother it will have a natural suppleness, one that we must strive to keep; but what about us? We do not need to go on a keep-fit regime just to enable our dogs to recognize leadership but we do need to be able to maintain a flow throughout our initial training. Body movements need to be graceful and quiet for their optimum recognition by the dog; we know dogs recognize aggression by body language, they also recognize strength and weakness by body language; but they are also unbelievably graceful when they are interacting with each other and the pack leader is no exception. In fact, if he can gain authority by being quiet and graceful, the greater is his power, for with his authority also comes an air of mystery.

Dogs are wonderfully supple and their bodies sometimes appear almost to flow from one direction to another. We need to try and emulate a little of that freedom of movement when we are training, because if our body is stilted, we are speaking in a stilted accent to the dog. If our body language is flowing and gentle then so is our dog 'language'. These dogs are having great fun in the water, they are old enough to know how to play correctly without harming each other and they will flow from one move to another effortlessly.

Dogs growl and make a noise when they are issuing warnings or when they are fighting, but dogs are also prepared physically to fight. Noise can be seen as the beginning of a threat of physical contact, therefore harsh and abrupt body language could be interpreted as a loud and threatening language. If a human is physically aggressive with a dog that animal will begin to see human weaknesses, for in the pack the leader should be revered and will not expect to have to show aggression. If it does, it will show it only once and then the young insubordinate will be expected to adhere to the rules. The insubordinate will also know that if it steps out of line again it may risk a fight which, if lost, could leave it severely injured and, if it survives, it could be cast out of the pack. We tend to allow misdemeanours to go too far in the first place and then, because we are humans, we will not follow through, as the canine leader would be expected to do.

To take control it is essential that your authority is quiet and does not resort to violence; for example, 'scruffing' a dog is tantamount to a fight but what happens if you lose? Apart from the fact that you have failed to master the dog, you may also have been bitten. If you win, the dog will see you as a leader because you are physically stronger, but it will also see a mental weakness in you. The quieter you are the more attention your dog will need to give in order to hear you; the more you can show a fluid strength in your movements the more your dog will listen to your body language.

Different Breeds with a Universal Language

We may have different languages according to our countries of origin, but we all have similar actions: we all drink, eat, work, play and sleep. Although we may have a different vocal language for our actions, if we were to use body language there would be far more agreement in them. Similar signs would be indicative of drinking, sleeping and eating; anger would induce a cross expression and pleasure would produce a smile. Dogs come in all shapes and sizes and in many different breeds, but, like us, they all share a universal body language. As puppies their mothers will teach them all good manners and cleanliness. They will have learnt to follow behind her for safety, to hide in the den when there appears to be a threat, to keep the den clean, and they will have played 'survival games' within the litter – games which may differ in style according to breed but are arousing the survival instinct. In fact, just like children they will have been educated in the way of the family and this will prepare them for life with the pack. This education becomes instinctive and is something they recognize, so that when they enter a human 'pack' they will expect to see similar 'language' from the new pack leader. From the smallest of breeds to the largest they will all expect the same kind of pack management. You may want to teach your dog all kinds of tricks and games, you may want to teach it many different words, but before you teach it how to understand humans you must first understand the dog within him and this means speaking his language.

Although all dogs have an instinctive knowledge of body language they will develop their own personal actions as they learn to identify with their pack leader. Learning the general body language of dogs and understanding what they expect is similar to learning a language without an accent. To fully understand your own dog you will need to study it carefully and to learn its own personal accent, for as it develops it will widen its vocabulary to enable it to have longer 'conversations' with you. If you are used to one particular breed you will be familiar with many of its natural actions, but if you have two different breeds it will soon become obvious that their actions will differ slightly but they will still convey the same message. A dog with a long tail will wag it when it is happy, but that does not mean that a dog with only a very short tail cannot convey the same message. A German Shepherd can look very alert and keen with its ears pricked up but that does not mean that a spaniel is incapable of the same expression. Different 'accents' but the same message.

Many of the smaller breeds of dogs have short, sharp body movements, for

Dogs have a universal body language, but different breeds have different shapes and this makes the language almost appear to have different accents. For example, Texas pricks his ears and immediately you recognize an alert expression.

usually as sharp but their body language is often very definite.

Understanding and using body language to communicate with your dog will help not only to interact with it but also to train it, for by 'speaking' with your body at the correct speed your dog will immediately know your mood. A dog in a pack will interact with the other dogs, they will learn by observing and then by joining in; your dog will be observing you and so if your movements are excited and your arms are making exaggerated gestures you will appear to be 'shouting'. Your dog can read one of two messages into this: you are either displeased or you are excited. If you are displeased he will not be sure what to expect of you nor what you expect of him, for if the pack leader were displeased he would not make a lot of noise but would assert his authority quietly but firmly. If a member of the pack or a litter mate were displeased then there might be some noise and maybe even a fight, so which category do you fit into? If you are excited then there has to be a reason for it, such as a wild, mad game or maybe a fun free-for-all with other pack members, so he will respond by mimicking your excitement. If we remember the reason for his thinking of excitement as a mad game with other pack members, we shall also realize that he is not associating this with anything serious. Teaching him something in a simple, quick and easily understandable way has now just gone out of the window. When it comes to advanced training with your dog then you can add, subtract, exaggerate or omit your body language, but you have to advance to this stage, it does not just happen.

Body movement may unwittingly transmit the wrong message to a dog and

example, the Jack Russell. Some of the medium breeds are capable of quick movements but may also be both fast and graceful; Springer Spaniels and Border Collies are two classic examples and both are still recognized working breeds. Larger breeds are obviously heavier and their movements are not

Webster does not have pricked ears but his 'accent' is quite clearly stating that he is alert.

without the handler even realizing it. We now know that a dog not only likes but needs its own space and that it may feel unsafe if this space is threatened. A dog who is an established member of your pack (you need only one dog to have a pack) and feels safe in your protection will rarely feel threatened, but this feeling of security comes with confidence. A young dog or a rescue will be depending on you for protection and you may not even notice the threat to the dog when a stranger advances a little too close, or worse, leans toward the dog. This simple action of body language may make the dog feel unsure, for it is an invasion of its space and it will be looking to you for protection. Where are you? If you are standing a distance away from the dog it must make its own decision about how to handle the situation. If you are standing at the side of the dog you are not offering protection. If you are bending down trying to soothe the dog and maybe stop it from growling or barking it will appear to him that you are actually condoning and encouraging him to protect himself. You need to be between the 'threat' and your dog to offer him the protection he would expect from a reliable leader and then you will remove the 'threat' by asking the person concerned to give your dog a little more space.

Another dog is approaching and your dog is showing signs of aggression, what do your do? If you take hold of your dog and shout or use what to your dog appears to be excited movements, then he will assume that you also are concerned by the approaching dog and you also are prepared to stand your ground. If you quietly move between your dog and the 'threat' and then carry on about your business as if the other dog does not deserve your attention, then your dog will follow you past the 'threat' and once again you will have proved your credibility as a pack leader.

Not all dogs will have a problem with oncoming dogs or with strangers, and not all will take advantage of a human being who does not appear to be a natural pack leader. But all young dogs need to be able to have something familiar to cling to and all rescues need to be able to have someone they can recognize as being dependable. Most people taking a dog home for the first time, especially a puppy, will ask for something familiar to the dog to take with them, it may be some bedding or a particular piece of cloth. But this will be the only thing the dog can recognize if there is no familiar movement

A dog's body language will tell you immediately if he feels vulnerable, and you should protect him and make sure that his 'space' is not invaded. Rex is intrigued by whoever is approaching, but his body has a slightly defensive tension, showing that he does not want his space to be invaded.

Rex is now clearly uncertain; the stranger approaching is not only entering his space but is walking immediately to the front of him. He has no option if he is nervous either to turn submissive or to retaliate with a growl. The stranger may not be aware of what he is doing, but Rex now needs his pack leader to intervene and stand between him and the offender in order to make him feel less threatened.

or pack order to observe. Most young dogs will settle quickly if they have something familiar around them, but we rarely give much thought to what the dog will expect from us, we lean more towards what we think they should expect from us.

The Stranger in Your Home

What does your new dog or puppy think of the people who visit your home and what do these visitors say with their body language? When a new puppy leaves its mother's nest and is taken to a new home where everything is strange it needs to feel secure; this is not possible if it is suddenly the centre of everyone's attention. Strangers talking loudly, children running, telephones ringing, television, radio, cats, pet birds – it is a new world full of new noises and can be quite frightening. The first thing it needs to know is that you are going to protect it – its mother would not have handed it over to any other dog that happened to be passing her home! Allow it to learn where it can be safe and to know who is part of its pack and who is not; allow it to take its time, there is no rush.

A rescue or older dog will not be spending most of the day sleeping as a puppy would, so it will be aware of who comes and goes all day. If people keep invading its space, leaning toward it, extending their hands, looking directly at it, standing in front of it, all language that the dog can see as a threat, you risk alienating it toward you before you have had the chance to show it that you are trustworthy.

It takes time to learn any language and if you want to understand your dog, see his point of view and find out how he views the world and what he expects of you, then you must study his language and teach him yours at a very slow pace. Never rush and never try to make things too complicated. If your dog shows by his actions that he does not like someone in his space, even that someone happens to be your closest friend, then respect his wishes. In time you may find that you can discuss the matter again and that, for your sake, he is willing to be a little more polite.

Chapter Summary

The pack leader should always be as quiet as possible, with both their body movements and voice. Shouting, growling and shaking your dog will be seen by it as aggressive. This may cause extreme nervousness, stubbornness or aggression, depending on the dog's character. Dog breeds vary in shape and size, but all dogs share a universal body language that they recognize. All know what to expect of a pack leader. Always try to keep your movements smooth and even so that you do not induce unnecessary excitement in a young, untrained dog.

CHAPTER 6

Whose Territory?

It is important to establish as soon as possible who is pack leader and what the pack rules are. If you wait, you will not only lose valuable bonding time with your dog but you will also lose credibility as a potential leader. Bonding with your dog is important, but it is impossible to bond with a dog that is always too busy to spend time with you; your dog should drop everything to be with you when you are available. You should be the most important thing in his life, but he will not elevate you to that position as a matter of course, for no matter how much he may feel that he needs a pack leader you must qualify for that position in his eyes.

A new dog will assess its surroundings and, if allowed, will decide for itself what role it intends to take, what position in the pack it will have, and who will own the territory. A new puppy will not be so assuming for it has just left the protection of its own family and will be looking for someone to provide it with security. However, if it is not provided with a recognizable leader it will have to provide its own protection and this will in time lead it to assume the role of pack leader.

To begin with let us take a look at an animal in the wild that, for whatever reason, has been denied the security and protection of a pack. It will be drawn to a pack of its own kind and will follow behind trying not to draw attention to itself and hoping that it will be safe in its shadow. The main body of the pack will not welcome it but neither will they trouble themselves to acknowledge it, providing that it remains at a distance and does not become a threat. If eventually the hanger-on can prove that it may be a useful team member, then it may stand a chance of being acknowledged and may even be allowed to enter the pack area.

This scenario is kept simple for the purpose of explaining the principle of what a dog will expect when it joins your 'pack'. It is important to remember that the dog trying to ingratiate itself, will be following its own kind; it chooses to do so and it can also choose to leave and to stay alone. The modern dog in the domestic environment (work or pet) does not have these choices and is certainly not moving in with its own recognizable kind. It does not knock on the door and ask to join the human pack, it is taken there and is introduced to many sounds and smells that are alien to its nature. All the more reason therefore for us to try and understand what it would expect, what would make it comfortable and what would be familiar to it. This must be the way a dog would see it and not how a human may think the dog sees it.

It will understand if you are cautious about allowing it too much freedom, it will expect to earn any concessions and it will not expect to be allowed to make major decisions. Major decision-making is for the members who make the rules, the hierarchy. So your dog will expect you to tell him where he can go and where he must not, he will need to know where he can sleep and what area is his to be safe in. He will also need to know what areas are to be kept clean and where he can expect the freedom to play his own games in his way. If the human element does not provide the dog with the necessary information as soon as possible then good manners from the dog will be a long time in coming. But if the human element takes the time and trouble to explain everything in a simple and easy way as soon as possible, the dog will soon have its position in the pack clear in its mind and the two can get on with living together in harmony. After all, we would provide all such necessary information as soon as possible to a child.

House Rules

We have now learnt that a dog will not expect a new pack to welcome him with open arms, yet that is exactly what we do. He will not be surprised if he is ignored, yet we do the opposite. He will not expect to be made a fuss of, and that is the first thing we do. So how do we turn this around to provide the dog with recognizable information and keep ourselves happy? You are probably thinking that I am sounding as if I believe in zero tolerance, that I do not get fun from my dogs and that I am very strict. You are in for a surprise! I firmly believe that the sooner you can communicate with your dog, the sooner you can establish the necessary rules, then the sooner you can have serious fun with your dog.

House rules will differ for the many breeds of dog, but rules are rules and all dogs respect them. The only real difference between a St Bernard and a Pekinese is the size. They will differ in temperament, in attitude, in how they will need to be trained and handled, but you will not be carrying a St Bernard around in your arms and it will have great difficulty in sitting on your knee each night. But they are both still dogs. If someone wants a dog that will be happy to live indoors, will not crave to be jumping in all the puddles, will not pull them over and will not need to attend dog clubs and be socialized, then a smaller breed of dog is advisable. Just because it may not show the inclination for all these things does not mean that it would not enjoy them if it were brought up to do them; but neither will a smaller breed of dog suffer for not doing these things. A larger breed of dog, however, needs more exercise and will soon create havoc in the house if it is not dissuaded from using its pent-up energy within the family home. Dogs of a working breed will certainly not be the kind to be denied the freedom to do all the things that can cause human beings problems but to a dog can be sheer heaven. It is never easy cleaning a mud-bespattered dog, but to most of the working breeds it is equivalent to being in doggy heaven when covered in mud. All the more reason to make sure that we choose a breed and size of dog suitable to our lifestyle and available free time.

There are certain aspects of dog training that are not negotiable and certain aspects that are left open to negotiation; in the same manner, although a dog must be given its physical and mental boundaries within the home, so must these first be considered in the dog's best

A dog needs its own bed and this needs to be in a safe area free from intruders. There are many different types of bed available. Poppy is in a plastic one with a soft mat to lie on.

interest. For example, it could be foolish to take a forceful, non-negotiable stance that the dog must sleep in the entrance hall; this may be the most convenient place for the human element but in actual fact the dog will be denied all privacy and protection. In this instance the humans must be prepared to consider a place which the dog can retire to unchallenged and in safety.

So let us look at the rules we need to establish and how to apply them. To begin with you need somewhere for your dog to be able to call his own. I do not believe in invading the dog's bed, it is an intrusion on privacy and is encroaching upon his space. I firmly believe the dog should be entitled to own his own bed, for where can he can go for safety and peace and quiet if someone can enter his private space whenever he feels like it? A contented, well-mannered dog does not need to defend its bed, for if it trusts its pack leader it will trust them to remove unwanted visitors or, better still, not allow them there in the first place. If this bed can be adapted to be mobile then so much the better; so we are looking at a box, a cage, a plastic travelling kennel or anything that can be kept clean. It can then be taken in the car, on holiday, on visits and, in fact, anywhere that you wish to take your dog and know that he will always have a bit of home with him. If his bed is not one of the many cage varieties but instead is a standard type of dog bed, then it needs to be placed where the dog can feel secure and have one particular area in the house where it will go. The bed can be moved to different rooms for various reasons, but at night and in times of security it must have one particular

Monty is in a soft, fur-lined bed, but this is not to be recommended for a puppy as it is not as easy to clean and it may tempt the dog to chew.

place and it must be one that the dog feels safe and happy to be in. It is not unusual for someone bringing their dog home for the first time and, having gone to a great deal of time and effort to provide a cosy bed in a position they thought would be perfect, to find that their new and apparently obstinate little charge has different ideas entirely. This situation calls for a trip back to the drawing board and a change of plan; for, if your dog really cannot feel secure in the area provided, then you must find one in which he does. Of course, you are not going to give in to any demands to sleep on the sofa, and think twice about under the kitchen table or behind a chair, for what appears safe to him on day one may have strangers' feet under it and strangers on it on day two. So find a safe place that is acceptable to your dog and is not going to be vulnerable at a later date. A utility room is always one of the first choices, but if your utility room is also a walk-through then your dog will either be vulnerable or confused as to what it must guard. It is always useful for a dog to let you know when someone comes to the door; but if your dog is living by the door and barking at strangers it may also become protective of its bed. If the dog is now told-off for protecting its bed it will begin to regard it as an unsafe place to be, for you are making him give permission to strangers to enter his space.

Now with a suitable area and bed arranged you can begin the teaching of boundaries. Nobody wants a puppy to destroy their home, and yet it is surprising how many people will say, 'We've been lucky our dog chewed only a table leg, a couple of cushions, a pair of

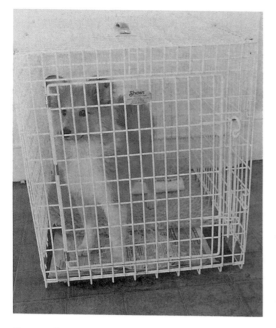

Barney has a cage which is ideal for a puppy; it can be used in the car and taken on holiday or when visiting friends, so the pup always has a part of his home with him.

and under your care, he has no right to pull it to pieces. Once he begins chewing and discovers what fun it is to reduce large objects in size he has begun on a downhill slide and so has your relationship, for there is nothing worse than opening the door and wondering just how much of your home is still in one piece. Naturally, you are going to be annoyed and this is going to cause more problems, for if your dog is chewing your 'kennel' (home) then he must be regarding it as his kennel and with him in charge of it, and so he wonders why you are annoyed. You should be doing what he wants not the other way round. How has your dog come to this conclusion? Because he was led to believe that he owned the territory. Would it not be a happier relationship if this did not happen? All you have to do is

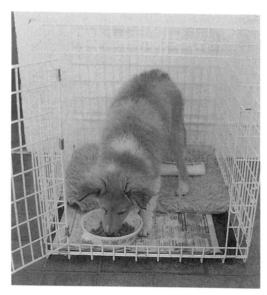

Barney's cage is his little home; he has his food and a bone. He will sit with the door open and happily chew his bone and has quickly learned that chewing in the house is not acceptable.

shoes and just one kitchen cabinet.' Some less 'fortunate' owners may have had a whole kitchen destroyed, plus a couple of carpets and maybe even a three-piece suite. Those who have had better control may be really happy to have forfeited only a pair of shoes. I wonder whether we would be as happy to settle for this kind of destruction from children? The degree of damage, of course, will always be relevant to the size and the breed of dog. A miniature poodle will take forever to reduce a kitchen to sawdust but you can rely on a German Shepherd, collie or any of the larger breeds to accomplish this task competently while you are buying the groceries. But why settle for your dog destroying anything? He is in your home

Mother will have taught her brood to follow her, so that when puppies do not have her to follow they will look for a substitute leader. These little ones quickly learned to follow my boots wherever I went when mum was taking a break.

to make sure that the dog understands that he owns his bed but everything else is yours.

When you first take your puppy into your home you will want to spend time with him, so all the more reason to make sure that, when you have finished this quality time together, he goes into his own 'kennel' to rest. Make a special effort to be on hand when he awakes and 'invite' him into your 'kennel'; this is such a simple procedure, but if your puppy can leave its kennel and go into yours whenever it wants to then there is no boundary between the two. If, however, you make a point of making him pause for a second in his own 'kennel' (and it need only be for a second) by placing your hand gently on him, asking him to wait and then allow him into your space then you have defined the boundary. You will not need to do this very often before he can come and go as he pleases because you allow him to do so. He has his own little domain and you have yours. What a wonderful foundation this lays, and in the nicest, kindest, gentlest way. He should respect and not destroy your area and he should not take advantage in it, nor should he soil it, and when he tells you there is a stranger at the door he will wait for you to attend to him. Only if you are not there will he make a decision about strangers in the house. He will protect and guard but always within reason. It sounds like the perfect dog, does it not? And all it takes is the establishing of who is the leader and who owns what.

If you follow the rule of 'pack' and give a puppy body language it recognizes, teaching it to walk behind you will not be necessary because it will automatically do it. It will then see the human as its pack leader, making the teaching of good manners very easy.

How Boundaries Work

A good canine mother will look after her offspring, protect them and teach them manners. As soon as they are old enough to be aware of what they are doing they are not allowed to soil the sleeping area; any species looks after its environment and the pups are educated to keep the 'home' area clean and tidy, according to dog standards. They will then automatically follow mum wherever she goes within this area; but when she is leaving the area she will increase her speed and when the distance from her is greater than the distance from 'home' the puppies will return to the 'den'. Try this with a puppy, and as soon as you are out of the protective distance or when the puppy is not in your pack space, it will return to

the only other safety it has, its home. This is your puppy telling you that it needs security and that it needs a 'safe house' of its own.

If you are dealing with an older dog then it will probably think that it can make its own rules. The behaviour just described is a natural reaction in the young, and so it is in the instinct of the older dog, he just wants to turn the tables on you, that is all. So you must make sure that during the first few days you are quite adamant about the older dog learning and respecting your rules. He will respect you for it and then you are already on your way to educating him into your pack.

So your new charge has been given his own bed and this is situated in a protected area and one that is acceptable to you both. An older dog will have an idea of where he wants to 'live', so it is for the two of you to find a compatible area. A puppy will not be capable of finding a place that is suitable as it has not yet enough experience of life to know how to select a permanently safe area, it will merely run for the nearest form of protection. You are already establishing, through your action of making the dog wait for a second before entering your home 'kennel', that you control the main pack area. That automatically makes you hierarchy and your dog is already learning good manners.

I would like to make clear at this point that I can guide but I am not making the rules, it is your home and your rules; I can only explain what the dog understands and so it is for the individual to decide when the rules can be relaxed. For example, we teach children not to push through doors, but we do not stop them and make them wait every time they go through them. Once the child understands the concept of good manners you can live in the grey area. It is for each individual to decide when and where the grey area, the area where you are living in respect and harmony, begins and ends.

If you fail to explain to your dog how your pack works when he first joins you then you could be making a rod for your own back. In fact, you will be leaving areas uncovered that the dog needs to understand, for even the dog which appears to know instinctively what is required of it and seems to take very little training will have an area that it is in control of. The most common areas for a dog's assuming control are pulling on the lead, failing to come when called, jumping up at visitors, aggression toward other dogs and chasing. The list is far longer

but these are the most common; a dog which assumes control in all these areas is definitely in charge of its humans and will be showing few if any good manners. Some dogs may appear to be both respectful and well-mannered in some of the areas and assume control in others. Some dogs may assume control in only one area. If a dog assumes control in any area, be it all of them or one, it is not a dog to be relied upon, for at some time and very subtly it will begin to extend its control.

The mother will tell her litter what she wants of them; they will not soil the bed but on most occasions she will not need to reorganize their toilet habits, as natural instinct will dictate where they go. They will be allowed to play and interact with each other and generally amuse themselves. They will not be allowed to wander more than a few yards from her protection and she will soon have them returned to base if they try to do so. She is their protection, she knows it and they know it. Now this scene has just set your first rule of boundaries for a puppy entering your home. Let us examine what the mother would allow and her three rules. A puppy needs somewhere 'natural' for its toilet area, somewhere it can 'recognize'. Paper is not recognizable and if the one on the floor is for the dog and one on the chair is for reading the dog may not understand this concept, and, if the one on the chair falls to the floor, why not use it? It is not unusual for a puppy to go out of its way to wet the Sunday papers and then sit with a huge grin on its face believing that you will be amazed at its ingenuity. Paper also leaves a smell that you may think you have eliminated, but your dog will still be aware of it, and so will visiting dogs. Go for a litter tray (the smell will not seep

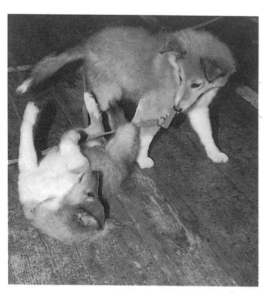

In the wild puppies will interact with each other naturally, this is how they develop. They also have an interaction with older pack members, this is how they learn. If you allow your dogs to interact without your guidance they will become a closed unit, they will recognize each other's body language and, apart from feeding time, you may find that you are surplus to requirements. It is often wiser to educate one dog before you get another; but if you do get two together remember to give them time with you as individuals and not always together. They need to develop into your pack and not to form one of their own.

through) and use soil, sand or any other substance that your dog will identify with the outside. Some people use litter but puppies may often be tempted to eat it, so be careful. Watch for your puppy's obvious body language and gently place him where he needs to go. I would advise that, whenever circumstances allow it, take your puppy outside, show him where to go and let him get on with it. Whatever you choose to use inside it should only be for use when your puppy needs to go little and often; it is not a substitute for the great outdoors, and do not make the mistake of following your puppy around with the tray and making it easy for him. He would have to make sure he went to the correct spot in his mother's 'home'. I have seen puppies come pouring out of mother's area in the morning and all run and line up in 'their' corner, so always try to keep the mother's good training ongoing.

The puppies will play with each other, they will have disagreements and they will have fun but they will also spend time alone. If a litter of puppies is observed closely they will be seen to be a little inquisitive (investigating each other's discoveries), they will run and roll and dig, not just together but independently, and, if tired, a puppy will quite often curl up and go to sleep on its own. They are a small pack, they are gregarious, they are a unit but they are also individuals and can be content with their own company when the mood takes them.

A puppy needs interaction from its pack, so you need to interact with it; but you must also be aware that it is perfectly capable of amusing itself, and not at the expense of your furniture, it is also natural for it to spend time quietly and doing nothing. A dog does not learn to use its brain if it is forever on the go, and if a puppy is always being encouraged to be doing, rather than thinking, then it will be conditioned to always having to be entertained. Allow it to develop its own games and allow it time to its own thoughts.

Now to the mother's strict and natural instinct for her brood. They are not allowed to wander from her protective area and, what is more, her puppies will not feel safe outside that area. So, rather than allow the puppy to wander a distance and risk its being frightened or hurt, keep it restricted to a safe distance until, first, it is more confident and, secondly, you have control of it. To begin with, a puppy will want to follow you and it will never be far away. You have to find a happy medium, for you have to educate it that its bed is its own safe area, the house and any immediate land outside, such as a yard or garden, are pack area and under your protection. Your pack (your dog) is not allowed outside your pack area and must not cross that boundary without your permission.

Teaching a puppy these pack rules is not difficult if you are consistent. Teaching an older dog will not be as easy, for it will probably already have decided upon its own rules and, if it is a rescue, it will have come to you with a fair amount of problem baggage. However, it is equally important to be consistent with an older or rescue dog, for he needs to know there is a secure area within your pack for him to be able to recognize you as a potential leader.

You must teach your dog physical boundaries and the perimeter of your pack area. If a dog is allowed to patrol the garden fence he will assume ownership of it and this can lead to barking, jumping up and eventually to his escaping.

'Where and What Can I Chew?'

The natural education of your puppy has now established certain recognizable rules. He has a bed of his own where he can feel safe and secure, he has been told what areas he may and may not soil, and, as he begins serious investigation of his surroundings, the pack area and its boundaries are made clear to him. There will be more little areas of education that you are covering as you go on and you will be making your own rules to suit your lifestyle. What we are covering in this book are the more essential points of behaviour, the ones that can create the foundation for a well-mannered, respectful and contented dog so that future training, for whatever purpose, is a pleasure. You also have to fine-tune these rules according to the breed and size of your dog. For instance, it may not be practicable for a toy breed puppy to go out on a wild, windy day when he has a perfectly

You may think that you have made your garden secure, but a puppy or small dog could prove you are wrong.

One small step for man, but a whole new world awaits this little dog. It could be exciting or it could be full of frightening experiences that it might never forget.

good litter tray inside. When he reaches maturity, although he may have outgrown the need for his tray, his size would still enable him to use it without creating problems for the human pack members. A larger breed of puppy needs to be encouraged to go outside whenever possible, and weaning from the litter tray (or whatever he is used to using) as soon as possible is essential; a large dog using your house as a toilet is no joke.

A smaller breed of dog can find a 'safe area' where a larger breed would not be able to fit as it grows, and a smaller breed of dog can take longer to investigate the outer boundaries, such as the garden fence. But be aware that, if you have a small breed and it is adventurous, it can soon disappear through the smallest gap in a fence and is not as easy to see when it is in long grass.

With the important rules of boundary on their way to being established and your puppy beginning to feel confident and craving to get on with doing things which are inborn, he will want to experiment with his teeth. This is a natural way of his not only teething but of preparing himself for future independence from his mother's 'table' and for being a useful pack member when hunting. Now do you want your dog to hunt and kill? Is it going to have to fend for itself? Do you want it to believe that it is correct for it to bite and chew and make decisions for itself regarding the right to bite? Your answers to these questions are not likely to take much working out. We know your dog is not going to hunt and kill, no dog needs these instincts to be aroused, not even working dogs. Gun dogs are no good if they kill; sheepdogs are no good if they kill. There is no conceivable reason why a dog should be educated to use its teeth for any reason other than chewing bones or whatever you provide it with to teeth on.

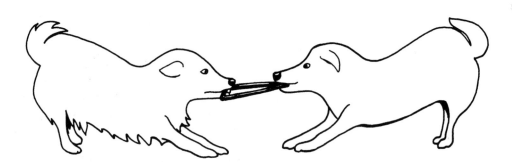

Puppies will tug to gain possession, this is part of their natural education and is arousing the instincts that will help them to catch and kill in the wild to enable them to survive. It teaches them how to use their teeth and young dogs will fight to gain possession. Therefore, to enable the young dogs to channel their instincts correctly, senior pack members supervise this education. We provide food for our dogs so they do not need to use their survival techniques and human guidance is not the same as senior pack member guidance, we are not teaching them to kill. There are many educational 'games' to play with a young dog without using games that will awaken an instinct that encourages it to use its teeth.

If any dog is to be educated to use its teeth it must be for specialized reasons and with specialized training. Your dog does not need to fend for itself; it has you as its pack leader and to look after it. If it is allowed to chew things in your home and if it is allowed to bite, then as it grows older it will make its own decisions as to when to use its teeth. So any experimenting your dog does with its teeth must be with your permission.

You can now fall back on that wonderful foundation of good manners you are creating in your puppy. For by educating him to wait a second before leaving his bed and entering your home you have also taught him to respect your home. As he grows in confidence so must you keep a check on his manners; if you think they are slipping a little, make him ask permission to enter your home from his bed a few times. The freedom of the pack area must be earned and respected. Now decide what you are going to allow him to chew; personally I prefer bones, they are what a dog would use in natural circumstances and they keep its teeth healthy and strong. Do not use uncooked bones or bones that splinter; most pet shops sell roasted bones that come in all sizes so they can be given to both large and small dogs. Some dogs may have a reaction to bones that does not trouble them but may trouble whoever cleans up after them, so remember that what works for one may not work for another. Whatever you decide to provide your dog with, make sure that it is not a replica of something he can find elsewhere in your house, for example, a dog chew in the shape of a slipper. You may know what you intend your dog to chew, but can you make it quite clear to him? If he has an old trainer or something that looks like a shoe, he

If you give your puppy an old slipper or trainer to chew don't be annoyed with him if he chews your best shoes.

may chew a good trainer or your best shoes. All you need to do now is to tell him where he can and cannot chew it. Your foundation of manners is teaching him that he has the freedom of your home with your permission and that he must respect your home, so now you must explain that he cannot chew in your home. Give him his bone or substitute in his bed, and if he leaves his bed bringing his bone with him gently put him back in it. If he leaves his bed and leaves his bone behind that is acceptable; if he leaves his bed and looks for something else to chew that is not acceptable. You are explaining to him that he has one thing only that he is allowed to chew and he is allowed to chew it only in his own domain. If you introduce your puppy in the first two weeks to the golden rules of 'when you have the freedom of my house it is only with my permission and you do not chew anything in it', you have laid the foundation for a happy and well-mannered dog, and a home without teethmarks.

If it seems a little strict or if you feel that it calls for rather too much commitment to educate your puppy as to where and what to chew, try to imagine your lovable, little, fluffy bundle when it is a few months older. It will not still be a cute little puppy, sleeping as many hours as it is awake and with seemingly harmless teeth. It will be an adolescent dog and it will want the whole world to know that Fido still rules in all departments and not just in the ones you allow. What may have seemed harmless when he was a puppy could manifest itself as being dangerous when he is an adult. So think before you decide that your puppy does not need educating yet, for the sooner he knows how to conduct himself the sooner you can relax and enjoy his company. If you encourage him to use his teeth, if he has a variety of things to choose from when he is playing and if you have allowed him to chew in your domain then the chances are that he will take advantage of the word chew and begin to eat everything in sight. If he sits on the furniture, the bed and on the front seat in the car whenever he chooses, you may find yourself sitting on the floor, then sharing the bed with a dog worn out from commandeering the car. Think dog and make your rules clear and simple. There is nothing strict about good manners, they are a necessary part of educating your dog.

Once again, breed and size can determine just how flexible you are with the animal and what you are prepared to allow; but all dogs have teeth and, although a toy breed may not eat a whole kitchen unit, it can sure make it look untidy when it has finished sharpening its teeth on it.

Should Your Dog Have the Run of the House?

Yes, if you want. Possibly that answer has surprised you, for I do believe that many theories of dog training stipulate that the dog should not have the run of the house, it should not have a higher elevation than yourself and it should be fed after your meal and not before. I do not have such rules, the dogs in my house do have the run of it, I feed them when it is most convenient to me and I am not in the least bit concerned about their sitting higher than I am. I am the boss, and it is all with my permission.

So let us begin with the house: if you want your dog to sit on the furniture, to go upstairs, sleep on the bed, then that is acceptable to me, and I imagine that it will be too to your dog; it is your house and your dog and so you make the rules. But this freedom must be earned and is only allowed with your permission. There is a subtle difference between your dog having the run of your house, thinking that it owns it and your dog having the run of your house and knowing that you own it! You have already made a start by teaching your dog the rule of 'wait for permission to enter my house' in the first few days. As the weeks pass, the new puppy will be exploring all the avenues of ownership and so it is essential that you

Ellie knows that this is not her bed, but her handler has given her permission to sit on it; her body language is relaxed and is not possessive. You would not grant this kind of permission to a young dog until it has learned its manners and it respects both you and your pack area.

apply the golden wait-for-permission rule to other areas. For example, imagine that you are sitting enjoying a cup of tea and thinking that you would like to play a game with your dog; at that point it senses you looking at a ball and promptly brings it to you. If you play with it you are doing its bidding, so you need to take the ball and tell the dog to sit down quietly in its bed. When the dog has settled and stopped being demanding you can then give it permission to come and play with you and the ball. You are in control. If the dog pushes ahead into a room, that it knows you are going into, it is displaying bad manners and assuming ownership of the room. Make it wait for a moment.

Let us imagine that one evening you go into your sitting room and your dog is with you. You are watching television and your dog is no trouble, it is sitting somewhere of its own choosing and will either change position or remain in the same place all evening according to how it feels. Now if this is an older dog who knows your rules, is respectful of your property and well-mannered, there is no problem. But if the main player is either a 'problem' dog or a puppy then there is trouble brewing, for it is making its own decisions and is not giving you the courtesy of asking you how you feel about these decisions. To begin with, when you are educating a puppy (or any new pack

Harry spends some time on his mat in the sitting room; this reminds him of the pack area and how he must respect it.

member) to your rules you need to have a place in the room that the dog can recognize as its own. So take the dog's bed into the room or, and sometimes this is far easier, you can use the blanket or bedding that is normally in the bed and that the dog will associate with its own home. Now all you need to do is to ask your pup to sit on its bed for a few seconds and then give it permission to have the freedom of your room. This freedom will last as long as the puppy behaves and respects your property; if it behaves in an unruly manner or one in which you believe to be bad-mannered, then it must go and sit in its bed for a while until it has calmed down. Being sent to the bed is not a punishment

and never should be used as such; what you are in effect saying is, 'if you can't behave in the way I expect you to in my home, then you must go and sit in yours until you have thought it out.' Think of educating children: if their play is beginning to be out of control, if they are not showing respect for their parents or the family home, then their play will be stopped and quite often they will be sent to sit quietly until they remember their manners. When you spend time with your puppy in the evening either playing or just sharing quality time, vary how you terminate this period. If you have been spending quiet moments together then he will probably fall asleep by your side, but

If your dog does not behave in your pack space then he must spend some time in his own. This is not a punishment, it is a fact that he must learn. Never allow dogs to share or interchange beds; Poppy is unhappy that her space is being intruded upon and feels that she is being reprimanded for something she knows nothing about.

if you have been playing then think about asking him to spend a few moments in his bed to settle down. This will remind him that you have allowed him to join you in your own space and that you are the one in control.

When you leave one room to go to another one and he gets up to follow you, it is a lovely feeling knowing that he wants to be with you, but he must not presume that he can always go with you; if you are not careful he will be taking you. Make a point of occasionally stopping him and making him wait a few seconds before inviting him to follow you. Similarly if he takes no notice of your leaving the room, occasionally make him follow you. This way of education works and it does not need to become a ritual; all you are doing is making sure that every so often you are reminding your 'pack' that you are in charge and that the freedom of the house is only by invitation. The same applies if you allow your dog to go upstairs: being on the first floor does not make the dog hierarchy to a pack leader; you have given him permission to use the upstairs, subject to his behaviour. If he is on your bed it is by invitation, as long as you know that when you tell him

We see three small logs; a big dog sees three big logs and a small dog sees three huge logs! The same three but they will appear different according to the size of the onlooker. Imagine what a molehill will look like to an ant or a mouse, but we may not even notice its existence since it is so small. Try to remember that your dog will never see exactly what you see.

to get off he does it without argument and does not assume that he can use it whenever he wants. The bed is yours. I know of many dogs, my own included, which have the run of the house and sleep on the bed and are biddable, well-mannered animals. I have also given consultations to many owners whose dogs have the run of the house and sleep on the bed and are unruly hooligans, many of them even have the cheek to growl at their owners when they try to get into their own bed at night. The difference again is subtle, in the first example the dogs know full well who is pack leader and who owns the house, the bed included. In the second the dogs are in control and will keep on taking over more and more of the house until the owners lose any credibility of being pack leader.

So here I am talking about educating dogs and saying why not let your dog sleep on the bed? The rules are yours to make, but whatever they are they cannot all be made overnight. Your puppy must be allowed to take things on board slowly, so for the first few months of his life you will be teaching him your basic house rules, where he can sleep, eat, chew and so on. Only later, when you have established yourself as pack leader and he knows without a shadow of a doubt that the house is yours and he must ask permission to enter certain areas of it, can you begin to extend his boundaries. When he is well-mannered you can consider allowing him access to previously unknown areas such as the bedroom. Size and breed will, of course, dictate just how much freedom you are going to allow him and which areas must always be out of bounds. If you have a very large breed of puppy then the bed just may not be big enough when the dog is fully grown, and the bedroom may not be somewhere you will want him. Big dogs are heavy, they need lots of exercise whatever the weather and they take a lot of drying after a walk in the rain; this does not bode well for a potential bed partner. Small dogs do not usually come in covered in mud and even if they did cleaning them is not difficult, they take up little room and are light in weight. But whatever the breed of your puppy it is still a dog, and it still needs to know what your rules are and that you are pack leader. Whether you decide to give your dog access to the upstairs of your house or restrict it to the kitchen or utility room, all of those rooms belong to you and must be respected by your dog. I am not advocating that all dogs should have the run of the house; what I am saying is that having your dog upstairs or on the bed is not going to make him either badly behaved or bad-mannered. If a dog is bad-mannered it is not because of where it lives, it is because of what it has been allowed to think it owns. You must, however, remember that if a dog is kept outside in a run it is far more respectful of your house when you invite it in. If a dog is restricted to the kitchen or the utility room it will be more respectful towards the rest of your house if you give it permission to enter another room. These dogs will know that the house is yours, for they have access to it only with your permission. So if you are eventually going to give your dog regular access to more rooms in your house, then you must make a point to keep reminding him just who owns that house. It is often not noticed just how much a dog has subtly but positively taken over until it is too late and it has become bad-mannered.

Chapter Summary

It is important that your dog has its own bed in a safe area. In the first few days in its new home a dog will expect you to behave as a pack leader and that you will provide it with your pack rules. Your dog needs to know what it is allowed to chew and where it can chew it and as soon as possible you need to lay the foundation for good manners. Allowing your dog freedom of the house and access to upstairs does not make it bad-mannered; but allowing your dog to think that it owns these areas will not only make it bad-mannered but will allow it to assume leadership over you.

CHAPTER 7

The Importance of Leadership

Leadership is a fine balance between creating a partnership with your dog and being in control; if you are not careful, you can tip the balance and either harm a special relationship or your dog becomes the 'boss'. I would like to return to the bringing up of children. Although my children informed me that I gave them the 'look', we were and still are very close and the best of friends. But when they were small I had to be in control; this did not mean, however, that they could not make decisions nor question me. What it did mean was that I decided when they could make decisions, whether they could question a situation or whether they had to accept it. I made the rules and when they understood them we all lived by them in harmony; you could say that when I had established myself as the pack leader that my pack of two children caused me few problems. (But should you ever meet them don't tell them I said that...) The only difference between my 'pack' of dogs and my 'pack' of children was the language barrier. Once leadership is established the rules are easy to live by, but it is essential that your dog understands that you are in control.

I do not believe that it is possible to tell someone exactly how to train their dog, for, if it were, there would be no individ-uals. All owners would handle their dogs in the same way and the dogs would become stereotyped. But dogs are not machines, they all have feelings, instincts and thoughts so they will not all respond in the same way; if they did we would not find them such fun to live with. This is one of the many reasons why it is important to understand your dog and to try to imagine how he views life and what he both needs and expects of you. Just as we learn to live with other human beings and to practise a measure of give and take, so must we be prepared to give and take with our dogs. This may make training contradictory, for example, you must be in control and your dog should do as you say, but it may question you. It sounds contradictory, but if I were to take my dog near a busy road then it must stay by me and behave with no questions asked. If I were to play a game with a ball and the dog made it quite clear that it no longer wanted to play, then I would be more than happy to 'listen' to what it wanted to do.

When Not to Negotiate

So how can you reach this wonderful stage in your dog's education where it

Teach your dog always to listen for your recall command, but remember that noise and foliage can impair his hearing. Hope stands tall above the grass and can hear his handler talking to him.

knows when it can ask questions and when you are not prepared to give and take with it? You never negotiate on important issues; as far as I am concerned, when I recall my dog, tell it to stop, to stay or walk with me it must do it. I care not whether my dog is 500yd away and enjoying a really good scent – when I give a recall it must come. The 'big four' are not negotiable and they must have an immediate response, for, if not, you directly lose credibility as a leader and also your dog could be placed at risk. Unfortunately, this is not always apparent until it is too late; dog fights,

road accidents involving dogs, and sheep worrying are all frightening prospects and many such accidents could be prevented if the dogs involved could have been stopped or recalled instantly. If you negotiate just once on any of these four during the first few weeks of sharing your life with either a puppy or an older dog, then you will make the next stage of education harder for yourself. But I promise you that if you use your dog's instincts then the 'big four' become relatively easy to teach.

In the first few weeks after a puppy or an older dog enters your home we have

Bella can hardly see or be seen in the long grass and the sound of the insect life there plus the density of the foliage distorts the sound of her commands, causing her to look in the wrong direction.

made certain allowances or adjustments for the different breeds and sizes, but all breeds should have an instant recall, and I do mean instant. If a car is travelling along a road and a dog runs out in front of it, the driver will either hit the dog or swerve. It will not make any difference to the outcome whether the dog is a St Bernard, a poodle or any size in between, someone is likely to be hurt either physically or mentally.

If you are not your dog's pack leader it will not respect you, and if it does not respect you it will not see you as a leader, so each one is dependent on the other.

Once your dog respects you it will want to come back to you on the first recall, and respect is not gained by bullying, shouting or scruffing. Nor is it gained with a box full of toys, titbits or a ball. So far we have discussed how to make sure that your dog respects your house and does not treat it as though it were its own. While you are doing this you can begin to establish some basic form of communication for training that will allow you to be able to take your dog anywhere and in any company without fear of your losing control. All you need to train a puppy to respond immediately to the 'big four' is yourself armed with plenty of patience, quick reflexes and the determination not to be persuaded by your dog to negotiate. You do not need to be armed with plenty of titbits; you do not need a ball, toy, check chain or any other item that goes under the disguise of the term 'training aid'. For a young dog does not need a training aid; it needs to understand, and if every time it does as you wish it gets a treat, edible or otherwise, pushed in front of its nose it not only becomes distracted, it will be confused. For there you are telling it that you are the boss and that it must do as you say, and the next minute it is holding you up to ransom for a game with a toy.

Toys

People often say to me, 'I know you don't like toys, but...' This is usually finished with any of the following, 'My dog will only come back for a toy', or '... will only walk with me for a toy', or '... enjoys it so I don't like saying no', or '... brings it with him of his own accord'. So who is the more important: the toy or the person? I am not against dogs having toys and I would not dream of preaching how owners should use these toys when interacting with their dogs, but I would hate to think that my dogs put a piece of squeaky rubber on a higher plain of popularity than I am. If a person has to rely on toys and titbits to teach their dog good manners then they are not communicating; they are bribing, and when the bribes are in short supply so are the good manners.

To begin with let us look at toys in the home. If you supply your dog with plenty of them he may learn several bad habits. To demand that you change toys when he wants, to become overexcited when throwing them around the room (humans do not even need to participate), he can bark and growl at them and may even chew them. If he shows a preference for one particular toy it will accompany him on walks and his human will obligingly throw it around for him so as to continue the excitement. Or they may keep it in their pocket and only show it to the dog occasionally so that he has to keep running back to make sure that it is still there. What he may find difficult to learn is the ability to focus and to concentrate on one particular thing for any length of time, other than waiting for it to be thrown. He may also find it difficult to differentiate between his toys and yours and to be patient and to sit quietly and be content with his own company.

If there are plenty of toys to choose from he will inevitably try them all out, and quite often owners may be guilty of thinking that the dog needs a change and actually encouraging it to keep playing with different toys. If the dog is encouraged to keep playing with the toys and if throwing one in the air and chewing it is acceptable, then think what fun the dog can have when it has been on its own for only a short while. If a toy is taken on a walk then the dog is looking forward to playing with it; your dog may come back to the toy and may do as he is told but he is not showing any respect or good manners to his owner.

If your dog has toys on the floor and you pick them up and play with them your dog could be forgiven for believing that he has every right to play with your toys – the clothes on the heater, socks or anything you may leave within his reach. He does not need a box full of toys; he would not have them in the wild and

Harry is fifteen weeks old and would love two-year-old Peg to play with him, but Peg is not interested.

'Please Peg, just a little game.'

'Well, all right but not with the ball, we'll use your stick.'

'Not likely – you wouldn't play with the ball so you're not having my stick, so there!' Two dogs of the same breed with one being more mature than the other and they can play in harmony without fear of hurting each other.

many of the toys available actually encourage chewing. In the wild he would find his own amusements and he is capable of doing that within your pack area; but it is a mistake to think that you need to supply him with them in order to keep him occupied and to prevent him from chewing your home. He needs simple rules and ones that he can understand. His requirements are for something to keep his teeth strong, something to keep him occupied and somewhere to be peaceful. If he has something to chew and you have told him that he may only chew it in his own area then he has a simple rule. If you have provided him with something to chew then he also has something to keep him occupied so that he can sit quietly and peacefully in his bed chewing a bone or whatever you have provided and this will keep him occupied until he is tired and rests quietly. If a puppy is reared to understand this concept it will be a delight to be with, for it will not be demanding and excitable in your home, it will be treating it as the innermost pack area to be respected and peaceful in. The time for extra activity is outside where it has room to play and run.

Does this mean that when I rear a puppy it does not play with toys and it does not have any form of amusement in the house? No, but I keep everything quiet in the home. If I have a puppy I never tell it how to play a game, I allow it to work it out for itself. For example, if I roll a small ball towards a puppy it will probably be cautious, so I roll the ball quietly around and then I leave the pup to work it out. It will eventually realize that it can roll the ball for itself, so now I roll a second ball towards it and, in order to pick up the second ball, the pup must drop the first one. I immediately pick up the first ball. Now we continue the game of my taking the ball each time the puppy drops it in order to gain possession of the one I am rolling towards it, and all the time I am very quiet. It takes very little time for a smarty-pants to sit on ball number one while picking up ball number two, leaving me smiling at his cleverness. However, when I have tried to show owners this game they cannot resist making sharp, jerky movements with the ball, telling the dog to 'fetch' and raising their voices to an excited pitch. The effect on the puppy or dog is quite dramatic for it is jerking its head to keep an eye on the ball, it is on its feet and is ready to run instead of lying down and thinking it out. It may also be 'imitating' its owner by barking.

The kinds of game I play with a puppy or older dog are ones that stimulate its mind, encourage mental exercise instead of physical, leave it feeling relaxed rather than wound up and allow it to devise its own games. I do not need to go out and buy fresh supplies of entertainment for my pups, for whatever I use does not get chewed or lost and we always use the game for education. All dogs know how to play and they have their own games, so when human beings produce toys they are actually encouraging the dog to interact and play with them; but the dog needs to know the position of that human being in the pack first. Also I wonder whom the toys are for? It is rather like when we buy a child presents, we are often buying what we ourselves would love to play with. So before you go rushing out to buy your new puppy or dog a selection of toys, get to know him first and teach him that you are the most important thing in his life and not a bouncy, squeaky, piece of rubber. When your dog sees you as the one he wants to come back to, the one he will always be looking for and the one he wants to please, then is the time to play with whatever toys or games you choose.

Even when I am playing in the house with a small ball and encouraging my pup or dog to use its brains rather than its brawn, we play only when I want to and with my ball. My pup is allowed to play on his own with the ball, but only when I give permission, and if he begins to be demanding and boisterous then the ball is taken away and he must sit quietly and earn the right to have the ball lent to him again. In this way I am controlling my dog's behaviour, but I am also carrying through my commitment to this action. Many dog owners will 'own' the toys and give them to the dog only when they feel the time is right. But if the commitment of making sure that the dog behaves with the toy is not carried through then the dog may become excited and forget whose house he is in. If the owner 'owns' the toy and then interacts with the dog in a way that encourages it to become excited then they are, in fact, giving the dog permission to throw things around in their home. In this instance you must see it from the dog's point of view. If it has permission to throw toys around when you are there then it may find a 'toy' of yours when you are out, play to the point of excitement and then begin the downhill slide of chewing something. When you are out is the time when your dog should be taking 'time out' and either quietly chewing its bone (or substitute) or resting. No young dog should be left in a house for a time that would exceed its chewing on a bone and then resting.

How to Gain Your Dog's Respect

If you have maintained a steady commitment to making sure that your dog has both mental and physical boundaries in your home then you will already be gaining his respect of your property. However, he will not find it easy to respect or see someone as a leader if they negotiate with him rather than command him when it comes to basic rules and good manners. This brings us back to the 'big four' (stop, stay, recall and walk behind); you need to be able to stop your dog and this means sit, down, stand or whatever you choose to teach, but it must be clear that it is to be obeyed the first time and immediately. Sit and work out what you want your sounds to mean to your dog: requests can be questioned, commands cannot, but neither should be repeated. You may use a request sound to your dog and it may think before it responds, but you will not repeat the word. For example, if I say sit to my dog, for no apparent reason, it is non-negotiable as far as repetition is concerned, but I will not be put out if it hesitates long enough to question my instruction. It has the capacity within its mind to wonder what is going on, and we all want our dogs to use their brains, but I will not repeat the word, I will give a sharp 'now' (wonderful word) and the dog will jump to it. But if I use a 'down' it is with a command tone and the dog must do it immediately and not ask questions; it may still wonder why but it must do first and ask later. The 'now' sound can be any word you choose to use but must not be used in the same tone as the original request. Imagine a child again, the parent does not keep repeating in the same tone,

We see two dogs, grass and trees.

A third dog sees little apart from two more dogs, making it want to push to the front. Study your dogs when walking with more than one and allow them all the opportunity to see in front.

'Put your toys away', he or she will say it once and then probably follow up with a 'Do as I say now', and what a tone they will use! None of us is perfect and we all want some degree of flexibility in our training, and we shall all make mistakes and repeat ourselves, no matter how vigilant we try to be. It is so easy when preoccupied to say 'sit' to a dog that is pestering for attention and, as long as it stops pestering, to not follow through and actually make it sit. So it is essential that you make sure you have at least one command that your dog will do not only at the first time of being told to but will do it immediately. If you were thinking of competing in one of the disciplines when your dog is trained it would be sensible to choose your commands for everyday use carefully. However, do not worry too much for dogs can become condition-trained, which we shall look at later; this enables them to react differently to certain words when in conditioned circumstances.

You need to remember that your tone is very important; if you use 'bacon' and 'sausages' your dog will respond if you use the correct tone. Your stop command must be something you are comfortable with and one that cannot be confused with anything else; you could simply say stop, but your dog must do it.

I prefer training to be subliminal to begin with, for the dog does not and never will understand human language; we teach it that certain sounds have certain meanings in regard to actions. But just as the word 'leave' may have several meanings to us, it will mean only one thing to a dog. What the human being must do is to make sure that the dog does not believe it must hear the word several times before performing the action. I am well aware that it is possible to have a conversation with a dog and that it appears to understand all that is said. I am no exception to this communication, I often have a chat with my dogs and, of course, they pick up key sounds (words) and this enables them to know vaguely what I am talking about. The older the dog the closer the empathy between dog and owner and the larger the vocabulary the dog will have built; but if you try to teach a puppy a full dictionary before it has learned an instant recall then you are asking too much. It all takes time and patience and the best conversations are often the unplanned ones.

Training subliminally is easy; it simply means that when your dog thinks of an action you give it a sound for that action. For example, each time your dog lies down, tell it what it is doing. If you push your puppy's behind downwards when you want it to sit, it will resist and then the sound of sit is associated with resistance. Because this command is one that you are teaching in close proximity you will eventually achieve what you want. But when you come to teach at a distance it will not be as easy. So instead of pushing your puppy down, put your hand under its chin and gently tilt it upwards at the same time stroking your pup's back; it will think, 'I want to sit down' and as it sits down say, 'Sit'. If you do this

often your pup will associate the sound of 'sit' with sitting, so that when you say the word it thinks it should perform the action; all you have to do then is say, 'Good dog', and it will sit. When you know your puppy is putting the two together make sure that you do not negotiate, for it is often a temptation to ask the pup to sit then wait and see whether it does it and then ask again to give it a second chance. There are no second chances; if it does not sit the first time go to it and make it sit, then make it stay in that position for a minute to reinforce your authority. You can teach your pup the 'lie down' command in the same way; it will often lie down of its own accord and you can give it the sound; if you lie down on the floor it will lie beside you then give it the sound. If you are playing with it and you both take a rest and it lies down, give it the sound. 'Stay' is not as easy as it entails more commitment but it does not take long if you do not negotiate. It does not matter whether your dog sits or lies down, for not all dogs like sitting and not all like lying, so to begin teaching the 'stay' use the one the dog prefers. When your pup will sit or lie down hold him gently in that position by stroking him and telling him to stay, move quietly one step away and back again and keep him in the same position. If, when you teach the sit command you keep your puppy sitting until you give a break command, which can simply be 'okay', your pup will be used to waiting for permission to move, making the stay even easier. Always make sure that you are facing your dog when you teach the stay, for this is part of natural body language. If the pack leader faces a dog it would not advance into the leader's space unless invited to do so; you are the pack leader so as long as you keep facing him he should be hesitant to move forwards. You are using natural body language to teach your dog the sound; when it understands the meaning of the sound to the action you can then position your body differently as you wish.

If you are dealing with an older dog who is used to a lead you can hold him still with the lead, but never allow him to move without first giving permission. We humans are often guilty of over-commanding our dogs, we tell them to do something and repeat the command, whether it is necessary or not, and no sooner has the dog settled into that command than we give him another. Dogs do not speak with their silent language so it is better that we keep our voices to a minimal level to begin with.

Lead Walking

Once you have your dog sitting or lying down and staying when he is told to, lead walking is easy. He knows that he should walk behind his pack leader, but if you are willing to settle for second best then who is he to argue? You can work out how the dog sees it if you look at the whole situation rather than one of your teaching your dog not to pull on the lead. No dog should even consider pulling, but if you allow it then it becomes his way of life and while doing it he is in charge. If you look at a pack of dogs or a tribe of Indians where is the leader? He is in front and he is not going to settle for his pack or tribe being a head's length in front of him. Now where are most dogs when they are on a lead? They are in front. So 'dog sense' tells us that this is not what the dog would expect from a leader: he would expect to be behind.

This dog is clearly in charge: she is taking her owner for a walk and she is in control. There may not be the risk of a smaller dog's pulling someone over, but it will still be in control in its mind and no dog, large or small, should be the pack leader.

Can I now hear all those shouts of 'But I want my dog to walk in front for obedience competition.'? Or 'My dog pulls but it doesn't matter for he's only very small.' In the past I have even heard 'I didn't get a dog so that it could walk behind me, what's the point of having a dog if it can't run and play?' I could not agree more, but the gentleman who made this statement was visiting me for a consultation because his dog pulled, did not come back when called and was showing aggression to other dogs. Well, of course it was, it was in

The handler may have every intention of turning to her left but in the dog's mind she is telling her to follow her. There is no point in telling the dog to come to 'heel' while she is pulling for she will associate the command with the action of pulling.

charge. I am not advocating that your dog should always be behind you, but he must be made to realize that his place in your pack is behind you. You make all the decisions, so when he walks beside you, goes in front, for competition or to run and play, it is with your consent.

Let us look at how dogs are often taught to lead-walk. The lead is put on and the dog resists, eventually after some sulking or arguing it may set off in the direction you want to go. When you decide to teach some manners you may pull him back and say 'heel' and, of course, tell him that he is a good boy. But what is he a good boy for doing? Was it for coming back to your side or for pulling forwards in the first place? If I go inside the dog's head and pretend that I have just been pulled backwards and told that I am a good dog, then I would feel that I had to pull again to please you. Of course, I want to be in front so it is no hardship, but I cannot understand why you have to keep pulling me or why I might have a small chain around my neck which hurts when I pull, but if it pleases you, then so be it. Now, at what point have we actually said, 'You must not pull.' We have, in fact, taught the opposite. I usually study dogs, imagine how they see a situation and then put it to the test, and I have lost count of the number of dogs I retrain to the word 'behind', but when the word 'heel' is reintroduced the dog pulls. I also despaired when a dog trainer told me that dogs eventually get the message when they are tired of being pulled back. I would rather make it clear from the start where the dog should be, for this rule not only makes lead-walking pleasurable but it also reinforces who is pack leader. A dog who ceases to pull because he is weary or has a tight check chain on is not walking sensibly out of respect of the leader, it simply has no choice, but the inclination to lead is still there. It is rather like saying, 'My dog used to bite but it's okay now because it wears a muzzle.' It still wants to bite, but it just cannot; far better to reach the source of the biting and explain to the dog that it is out of order.

You need to explain to your dog that it must stay behind you and in your pack area until you invite it into your space. In

Instead of allowing your dog to go in front and having to pull it back, you need to teach it that it must stay behind you and keep in the pack position. In this way you are not only in control but you are telling it that you are the pack leader.

the case of a puppy, you will have already introduced it to the lead by allowing it to trail behind it in the house; however, the way you are teaching lead-walking will not make your puppy resist a lead even if it is not used to it. Tell the puppy or the older dog to sit and to stay, now move forwards almost to the end of the lead (your lead needs to be approximately 4ft long) and gently give him permission to move. This permission must not be granted with a tone of voice that leads the dog to believe that it is going to run free, so keep your voice quiet and make your dog expect something more to come. Now

before your dog reaches you, tell him to sit and stay again, wait a few seconds for him to think about it and then repeat the action, always keep your back to your dog. You are teaching more than just one thing for you will not be negotiating with either the sit or the stay command so you are reinforcing your position again. You are not allowing your dog to draw level with you, so you are retaining the leadership position and, although you may be watching him over your shoulder, you always have your back to him so he is in pack position. Do not give your dog a command for this action until he does it

When your dog respects you as pack leader you can invite it to come forward anytime you wish.

Sandra now has Skye under control; her dog understands its position in the pack and is able to come forward for free walking or for competition work.

correctly, hence the reason for only giving permission to move; when he is walking behind at a steady pace you will then use the sound you wish him to associate with this action. You will not need to keep making him sit, for after being made to sit a few times he will be slowing down behind you ready for the command and then is the time to say 'behind' or 'back' or whatever word you choose. If you use a word that you can associate with the action it is often easier to use and it leaves the 'heel' sound free for when you wish to draw your dog forwards into that position. This method of lead training is wonderful for a young dog as it never

learns the bad habit of pulling, and the older or rescue dog learns to concentrate on its owner rather than sniffing the grass verge and looking around. In fact, if you have a puppy you should hardly need to do this for in the house during the first few days he will want to follow you. All you have to do is give him the sound and, when he passes you, either turn around or pick him up and put him back 'behind' you. The method of changing direction will work with puppies for they are not fast enough to pass you, but it rarely works on older dogs for they misinterpret it as a game and try to beat you to the turn.

Recall

Now you have a dog that sits or lies down when you tell it, and on the first time of asking, and it walks sensibly on a lead. Remember that you are not negotiating on any of these commands: if your dog does not sit go to it and make it sit. If it breaks its stay do not ask it to sit again for it should not have moved in the first place, take it back to where it was and put it into a sit with your body language (hand under the chin) and tell it to stay. If it passes you or draws level with you on the lead without permission then make it go back behind you, you must give it permission to go in front. Listen to yourself all the time for it often becomes a habit to repeat commands and you cannot expect your dog to do it first time if you have not always insisted that it should. At this point may I remind you that we do not need to use either food or toys to accomplish this level of good manners. If your dog does something correctly and you give it a treat then you are breaking its concentration and it has to settle down to learn again; you are also informing it that it can expect a reward for good manners. It needs to know you are pleased with it, not that you think it needs feeding. A 'Good dog' is sufficient and once again your tone is important, for if you are using an excited tone then your dog will respond in a similar way and loses his concentration again. Use a smooth, gentle tone that also indicates that he must stay where he is. Think about the sounds you may be using, 'sit' is short and sharp, 'down' needs to be a tone lower and slightly longer, and 'stay' needs to be firm and quite a long sound. Now if you say 'Good dog' in a pleasant but long sound it is indicative of 'stay' as you are praising it rather than encouraging it to jump about. In a dog-to-dog situation one does not give food or a treat to another because it has abided by the pack rules, it is expected to adhere to these rules and thus will expect to be reprimanded if it is insubordinate.

A puppy is easy to teach a recall to, for it will never be far from you in the first few weeks, so every time it runs to you give it the sound you want it to associate with that action, and try not to keep using its name. If you were speaking to a person you would use their name to get their attention, but if they were looking at you they would know that you were addressing them by your body language and you would not use their name at the start of each sentence. If you keep using your dog's name unnecessarily the name will become part of each command and, as it will be the first sound the dog hears, you have wasted valuable seconds of reaction time with its name. If a dog is educated to listen for its owner's voice, it will answer to it and will not be running to 'sit', 'lie down' or recall whenever anyone else within earshot calls to their own dog. There are times when you will need to call your dog by its name so do not waste this strong attention-demanding sound by overuse. I am convinced that the human preference is for commands of more than one syllable and, as dogs respond better to tones, it is far easier to make each command have a different sound if it is lyrical. So instead of prefixing each command with the dog's name why not use 'Come here' or 'Come now' or 'To me' or 'Come on back', or the shepherd's universal command of 'That'll do' (very lyrical)? If you used 'hockey sticks' or 'bananas' (both lyrical sounds) your dog would respond if it heard it

The recall is not negotiable, a dog must come back the first time it is called and it must do it immediately.

Isn't this a wonderful photograph? Eric's expression is full of joy as he bounds back to his handler with a 'happy recall'.

every time it came running towards you. The secret is to make sure that your dog is wanting to come to you and then give it a lovely, lyrical sound that is music to its ears and cannot be mistaken for anything else. By lyrical I do not mean a high-pitched call because this will not carry on the wind without being distorted; it will also be difficult to obtain the same pitch each time, other family members may find it difficult to emulate and, when your dog is near to you, it will be far too loud for his ears. Talk to your dog with your commands and in your own voice, after all, that is the voice he hears every day, but make sure that your tone means that you expect attention.

A recall should be one of your dog's happiest commands and he should come running the instant he hears it. If you educate him to this sound in the first few weeks you will have few problems later, unless, of course, you negotiate. It goes like this: in the first few days puppy runs to owner and owner give the recall sound, in the next few days owner gives the recall sound and puppy thinks, 'I want to run to owner', then receives a 'good dog' and some attention. In the next few days owner recalls puppy, which now has almost got the concept but not completely, so when he does not respond immediately owner goes and takes him gently to the spot whence he first called him. The exercise is then repeated immediately for the dog to get the concept that to return is happy, not to return brings no response from the owner. Consistency is the key word and making sure that you do not fall into the trap of repeating your command or of telling your dog it is good when, in fact, it took far longer than it should have to respond to you. Expect a good response and be indignant if you do not get one and use natural body language.

If you face your dog when you call him, just as in the stay position, he will want to stop a yard in front of you; he will also be hesitant to recall to a leader who is facing him, for you are walking into the pack and he should disperse. Turn your back, walk away and, when you are sure that he is following you, give him the recall command, keeping your back to him until he is seated behind you. Tell him that he is a good lad, put on the lead and then you may face him. You may find that if you turn too soon he will retreat into the 'pack' or run into the pack space, and then you have wasted your recall command. If you are not sure that your dog is going to come, do not give the recall, for if you cannot follow through you cannot ensure an instant recall. Call his name – this is not a command and therefore can be repeated – when he gives his attention to you, call again and, when he moves to follow you at a run, give him the recall. All this is done in a confined and controllable area, until you know that you have control. The time to teach is when you know you have boundaries that are identifiable to your dog, and not in the great open spaces.

Now the older dog will probably not have had this kind of training, but it is not difficult to go back to basics and to teach an instant recall. First of all you can do exactly the same as in puppy training, and there is a wonderful advantage of teaching in this way for it can be done indoors in the evening or it can be done in the garden. If the older dog is not willing to come straight back, attach a long lead or piece of cord to his collar and, each time you call him, bring him gently but firmly toward you, keeping your back to him unless he knows the meaning of the recall. He now receives his 'good dog' and off he can go to play again. Keep repeating the exercise and make sure that, when he reaches you, he knows you are pleased with him. All this work is done at close quarters so that communication is clear and cannot be misunderstood; as well as teaching a recall this is also helping the two of you to build a relationship of respect and mutual understanding. It is what I call the 'feel-good factor', for each time the dog pleases you he receives a firm stroke from you and a tone in your voice that makes him feel you are proud and pleased (not over-excited) with him. It makes him feel good. If he were receiving a treat he would hardly notice you, instead he would be searching for his food or a toy and, on receiving it, would carry on with his own business and not care what you may have in store for him next (unless, of course, it involved another bit of food).

The Pack Area

Now we need to study the pack area, for it is a big mistake to take your dog out to a large expanse of grass and let him go running off without a care in the world. For if an aggressive dog were to appear there could be a problem; he would also have to make his own decision as to how to deal with this situation since he might be out of your pack area. Your pack base is your home and you have already taught your dog where the boundaries are; but

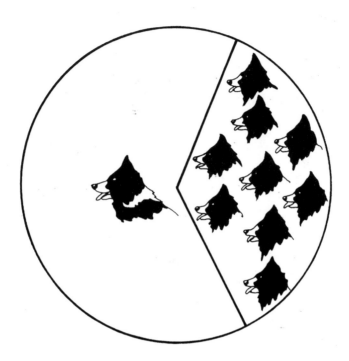

To teach your dog to walk correctly on a lead and to establish yourself as pack leader your dog must learn to understand his position in the pack, he will expect this of you and he will respect you for it. Imagine a circle approximately 25yd in diameter and yourself in the centre of it: this is your pack area. Look at the pack leader in the diagram moving forwards and in front, the rest of the pack is behind and the nearer they are to the perimeter the further behind the centre line they travel. The leader in front is the one who sees all and makes all decisions. The pack is not allowed to come forward without his permission. Your dog must be behind you to enable you to have complete control and to teach him with your body language that you make the decisions. He must learn to trust you and he must earn your trust before he can enter the space in front of you.

when you are on the move you will take a protective area with you. Imagine a circle approximately 25yd in diameter and yourself in the centre of it. Now you are walking forwards and the circle moves with you, so you never reach the perimeter and there is a line from your feet to the outer edge of the circle. This line is at a slight angle so that when it reaches the edge of the circle it is no longer level with you but slightly behind you, you are almost at the point of an arrow within the circle. Now your dog's area of close control is immediately behind you and it may move within your pack area (the circle) with your permission. So, when you need close control, it is behind you; when you are not sure what is ahead it may be given permission to have more freedom, but only in the pack area behind you. When you are strolling leisurely along with no apparent dangers, you can give your dog permission to use all the pack area, front and back. Your dog must not leave the pack area without your permission and only if it has an instant recall. When you have taught your dog that it has a pack area around you and that it must seek permission to enter certain areas of it, then you have taken control of the walk. Dogs will not make decisions on how to deal with approaching dogs or people when they have a reliable leader, for the pack leader makes those decisions.

You can now practise your recall within this circle and you can also reinforce the area by checking him with a 'wait' or a 'stop' command each time he nears the perimeter. When you are completely certain that your dog is responsive to you and will come back on the first time of asking every time you call then he has earned the right to go outside the pack area. But you must lengthen this area gradually with the stop or the wait just as you did inside the circle; in this way you will keep in contact with him all the time.

I feel quite sure that by now someone is sure to be saying, 'But my dog loves to run for miles and to chase rabbits and is

These dogs have been told by their handler to walk in 'pack position'. They are happy to trust their leader and to allow her to make any decisions about where to go and how to approach other dogs or people.

When the handler is satisfied that her pack will neither be in anyone's way nor be annoyed by other dogs, she gives them permission to have more freedom in her pack area. They are all happy and relaxed for they know they have a reliable pack leader.

always 200yd or more in front of me.' Fine, if you can call him back first time every time; if you cannot then he needs to go back to basics and to learn to take notice of you as his pack leader. I would hate anyone to think that I am depriving dogs of freedom with these rules, but, if you could see all the case histories of owners who have come to me for a consultation because they have a serious problem regarding their dog, you would realize the importance of control. Most involve chasing, running off and not coming back straightaway and displaying bad manners in general, which often leads to aggression. The problem has always become serious by the time they

reach me, but it could have been so different if only the instant recall had been employed from the start. Your dog can have freedom to run, but it must be under control and you must be able to bring it back under close control and the protection of your pack immediately, for its own sake and for the sake of others who may not want your dog's attentions. Dogs chase rabbits in the wild, not for fun but for survival, and, if you allow this as part of its exercise, it is being educated to chase because you are allowing it. Before long this kind of unintentional education can lead to car and bicycle chasing and eventually could even lead to chasing and biting another dog or a child.

It is at this stage that many owners begin to recognize a problem, and when I delve into the dog's past and explain how it has come to be a 'chaser' they begin to see the connection. The worst part of this kind of situation is that the dog believes it is not doing anything wrong, for it has always been allowed to make its own pack area and its own decisions and so it cannot understand why things should change just because it took a little nip. You may also be surprised to find that, if you educate your dog to your pack area and to falling in behind you if you are unsure of what lies ahead, when you do give it freedom to leave the pack area it will keep coming back to you for your company. Do you want your dog to be with you or do you want it running half a mile in front of you out of control? I know I love the company of my dogs and I also like to feel that they enjoy my company, and if I take them for a walk it is not so that I can be on my own while they are way ahead of me. I walk with them for some quality time together, just them and myself, and a quiet time to share some pleasant moments together. I also know that I have control of them and, when other dogs come running up, refusing to go back to their owners – and this happens far too often – that my dogs will sit and wait behind me until the other dogs have gone. This does not mean that my dogs have no thoughts on the matter; I know Hope would dearly love to give every female dog he sees a kiss and every male a growl. Skye would willingly shave every dog, male or female, with her teeth for daring to come too close, and Meg would prefer to run the other way.

These are only three different temperaments of the dogs I have, but I have used these because they are so different from each other. Hope and Skye know that they must not be aggressive or otherwise without my permission and Meg knows that, whatever the threat, she is safe in my pack area behind me, for I will not let anything harm her. I would also add that my dogs are perfectly sociable, but they are free to make their own decisions as to how they feel about other dogs; however, they are not free to act on those decisions without my permission. I will also not allow a strange dog into my pack area if my dogs are in the least bit uncertain of it or if it is showing aggression. My duty is to my dogs and I will show determination to prevent any threat from reaching them. I do not want my dogs to fight and I do not want to have to give them permission to fight and so therefore I must make the decision to prevent the offender from upsetting them. I will also have given them all individual consideration according to each one's temperament and character. Meg needed lots of gentle and reassuring voice praise when she was young. Hope needed to be told who was pack leader in no uncertain terms, but, for all his arrogant exterior, he is a very sensitive dog and therefore all his foundation training needed to be precise to ensure that he did not become confused. Skye loves to please to the point of presuming what I am going to say and doing it without permission, all very well until she decides to do something I was not even thinking about. It is this flexibility and sensitivity to the dog's temperament that develops its character, its humour and the empathy between the two of you. But all dogs still need the foundation of good manners and the non-negotiable, all-important, big four commands to ensure that they understand your place as the leader and their place in the pack.

Leadership Helps to Solve Problems

With the concept of leadership being understood, both dog and handler can step out with confidence, for any problems that may arise along the way will not alarm the pack who will be under the protection of a trustworthy leader. That first trip to the vet will be made when your puppy or dog trusts you and to a vet that you, as leader, have already spoken to and know that you can trust. Any nervousness that your dog may be feeling when he is in the waiting room will be overcome by your calm, reassuring but firm voice. If you keep saying 'Good dog' to your dog when he is nervous you are telling him that he is good to be nervous. Keep your voice normal and run through some of the basic sounds he is familiar with, tell him to sit, down and stay, keep talking to him and his attention will focus on you: now he is a 'good boy'. I know that there is a trend to take the favourite toy or a titbit to help in such situations but it almost seems like giving a dog a false idol: no biscuit or ball can offer protection, they are just diversions. The vet is still going to see your dog so allow the animal to put his trust and his focus on to you. There is no reason for him to be upset by a vaccination or a tablet and I have yet to have any of my dogs frightened by a needle. They will sit calmly with pricked-up ears in the waiting room and they never even notice that he has injected them or given them a pill. Your dog must be able to trust you and you must be able to trust your vet.

This calm but strong leadership is vital to your dog, for he can be faced with many new or worrying situations. I know that it is a temptation to take a new dog or puppy straight out into the big, wide world so that you may enjoy his company, but before you do, for his sake and yours, please give him a leader he can trust. All your foundation training can begin in the home; indeed, this is where it should be learnt. 'Never ask a dog to something 20yd away it won't do 10yd away.' This is one of the main principles of canine education, so, if your dog will not come to you in the garden, what chance have you of getting a recall out on the playing field? If you are consistent and show commitment in the first few days and weeks you will have a wonderful companion to take out, and, one must emphasize, a new dog or puppy needs to get to know his pack area and his leader before he ventures near other packs (dogs). Exercise for the first few days is mental and physical and lead-walking is essential for a new, older dog that does not have an instant recall until you have begun to create a foundation for your partnership.

Traffic, car horns, car headlights, dogs of different breed from yours, they may all be new and often frightening experiences; but if he trusts you and you remain calm and are between him and the offending 'creature' then he can learn to face the world with confidence. Remember not to exacerbate any problems by foreseeing them and telling him that they are there. For example, a handler can hear a lorry or see a large dog approaching and begins to tell his dog that everything is well and that he is a good dog. The dog will immediately wonder what is going on, will become nervous and transmit this nervousness back to the handler. The handler may now become concerned, for he will not know what the dog's final reaction will be, to turn and run, to stand and growl or to chase? By the time the

Where there's a will there's a way! Big dogs can climb and see the world around them but little dogs are compensated by being able to get where big dogs cannot, and dogs of different characters can be entertaining to watch. Hope is unaware of little Bella sneaking under the style just to his right.

'problem' has approached the dog has taken matters into its own paws and the handler now has a dog that reacts every time it sees a motor vehicle or an approaching dog.

If that same handler had done the proper foundation training not only would the dog have a leader it could trust but the handler would have known the dog well enough to have been able to anticipate its reaction and to act accordingly. He could have placed himself between his dog and the approaching problem and kept walking, using a normal voice. If it was not feasible to keep walking and the situation demanded that he stopped, then he could have put his dog through his paces, sit, down, stay and continued to talk normally; then, when the coast was clear, walked on as if nothing had happened, telling his dog what a good lad he was when he was calm and obedient.

Now, if a ball or toy is employed in a similar situation you are using what is called a diversion method of training. You

Medium-sized dogs are popular, big enough to take anywhere and not too big or strong, they are often a working breed and are quick-witted and full of fun, finding mischief in every corner. Kim thinks there is a rabbit under the hut and starts digging.

'One more pawful of soil, and rabbits here I come!'

'Oh no, did I hear someone calling me?'

are saying to your dog that, whenever a problem arises, it gets a treat and goes off in another direction, both physically and mentally. You are not telling it that there is not really a problem at all and you are not telling it that you are capable of looking after it. Let us look at another situation: there is a knock at the door, the dog jumps all over the visitor, maybe in a friendly manner or maybe with aggression, the handler throws something on the floor to distract the dog, then catches the dog and removes it to another room. The same technique can be used to 'divert' a dog showing aggression to other dogs or to people on a walk. This method of diversion is acceptable in the short term because it can prevent contact between the dog and the visitor or it can take its mind off aggression. But it is only a temporary diversion, for it will still react the same way when the same situation recurs. Diversion can work for some dogs, but it takes time and it does not make you into a pack leader. You are compromising, 'If you don't do that I will give you a treat', or in some cases you are offering a larger problem for the dog to deal with, 'If you do that I will make a nasty bang near you.'

You are a better leader to your pack if you do not allow it into the situation until you have explained the basic rules of good manners and the 'big four'. When someone knocks on the door (and this can be arranged with a family member or an understanding friend) the dog is told it is a good dog to bark; do not stop it from doing its job, but then it must sit in its own 'home' until you make a decision about the visitor. Make sure that you have the dog's bed or its bedding in a safe corner but in sight, tell your dog to sit in its bed and to stay there. When the visitor is settled the dog can come out and say hello, if you want it to. It takes practice and commitment, but once achieved your dog will respect you and you will find other 'problems' almost solve themselves as the dog falls into place in your pack.

There is little difference between the dog having bad manners at the door and being aggressive outside the home, for in each situation the same bad manners will be in evidence. The dog will believe it owns the home, and so in actual fact it does not see anything wrong in answering the door. The dog pulls on the lead, so it must make its own decisions, for it is in lead position and so sees nothing wrong if it decides to be aggressive. All the diversion and toys in the world are not going to give the dog the message it would expect to receive from you and understand as a dog: 'You are not the leader, I am!'

The different breeds will relate differently to our requirements. If you have a toy breed it will probably not want to go running off after rabbits half a mile away, and if there is any aggression on a walk it may be from other dogs towards yours. If your dog is on the floor you will still need to use the leadership position in front,

and, if you pick it up, use a firm and gentle tone or you will be telling him that you feel scared too. A large breed is far too strong to be allowed to pull, for it can not only do physical damage to a person's arm, your arm will be almost impossible to pull it back when it is at full strength. It must know its place in the pack and it must be under control, for a large dog showing aggression is a fearsome sight; many of the large breeds are big softies but one bite is enough to do serious damage to another dog or a person. Medium-sized dogs are the ones that I see most for consultations and problems for they are very misleading: popular because they are not too big nor too strong, but they are big enough to run, play and do the disciplines. But, can these dogs train their people! They are small and cute when pups and they are quite often of a working breed and so have quick minds, but in a very little time they have the whole household organized and then they begin to organize every other dog and human they see on a walk. These are the dogs that will chase rabbits, they will go for half a mile and not come back, they will jump all over other dogs and people and they are capable of making aggressive decisions. Unfortunately they have often established themselves as pack leaders by the time they have reached adolescence and their owners are suddenly faced with a fully-grown, wayward dog: a dog that demands that its owner should repeat everything half a dozen times at least, drags them on the end of a lead and terrorizes small dogs, cats and anything that looks like it could be fun to chase. All the games that seemed like fun at the time, chasing a ball, tuggy games, chewing and playing with squeaking toys, have, in fact, helped him to gain his new power, and he is not going to be demoted easily. If you play all human games and do not keep reminding your dog that he is a dog, he will grow up with confused instincts, he will never be a human, so before you try to teach him some human traits allow him to be happy with his own identity. So think dog and get *him* to think dog before you play human games and you will have a delightful companion to share your life with and you will be ready for the next stage of teaching your dog your language.

Chapter Summary

Your dog must stop, stay, walk behind and recall at the first command and immediately. You must never negotiate nor repeat these commands. Do not try to teach your dog advanced 'language' before it has learned the basics and make sure that you help him to understand what you are teaching by the correct use of body language. You can teach the foundation training and good manners in your own home and garden; never be tempted to test these commands outside the home until you are certain your dog understands them. If you are a good pack leader your dog will always look to you for guidance and this will help to overcome any potential traumas such as a trip to the vet, busy roads, aggressive dogs or dogs of different breeds.

CHAPTER 8

Word Association

You will introduce more and more words into your dog's vocabulary so you must be very careful how you select these and what you use them for. We humans are a funny lot; there is a saying that we should think before we speak, but we rarely do. I do activity days called the 'sheepdog experience' and this involves people who have never previously worked a sheepdog learning how to work a trained dog around sheep. There is a huge learning curve, for, although the idea was originally intended to provide information about sheepdogs, it has developed into an insight not just into a dog's mind but into people's characters and the way they train.

I have watched people call their dog to them several times and then eventually get down on the floor almost pleading with it to come to them, and, when it does eventually return, they tell it what a good dog it is. Now, having read the previous chapter you can see the mistake in this, and when I point it out to them they admit that they had not realized the implication of repetition. Then they begin working my dogs in a controlled area and over-commanding is apparent with nearly everyone, especially the stop command. My dogs know they should stop when told to but almost everyone who works them says the down command twice, automatically, and the second command follows the first without their even waiting to see whether the dog obeys the first one. Next time the dog will slow down at the first command and then will walk arrogantly forward, forcing the handler to repeat the command another twice. I have to say that the handlers take it in good part, but they also tend to see their own dogs in a very different light. What is evident on these activity days is the way handlers negotiate with their dogs, give them human body language and confused sounds. For example, most of the commands sound the same when they are talking to their own dogs: 'Fido sit', 'Fido down', 'Fido stay', 'Fido come.' They all sound the same, they are not very lyrical and they all begin with the same sound, Fido. When they use the name when commanding my dog, the dog will stop and look at them as if to say 'What?'. Which is exactly what I would do if someone called my name. Once you have your dog's attention it knows you are speaking to it, therefore it should not be necessary to keep using its name, its attention should be focused on you.

Another human 'habit' is to call the dog and then not take notice of the response, but instead to assume that we should keep talking. A good example of this was with a seven-months-old dog of my own breeding and belonging to a family who had worked really hard at teaching it the basics. They came to show me how well it was behaving and tried its recall, which was instant. But when the dog was halfway to the handler he called it again, very softly, to keep it focused on him and then called it again when it was only a matter of a few yards away. Of course, he made a fuss of it when it finally came to his side. But when he tried it again and I asked him not to speak a word after the first recall the dog got halfway to him and stopped. He had taught it to do this without realizing it. She is a wonderful little dog and her focus was totally on her handler so when she did not get the second and the third recall command, which earn her praise, she stopped and waited to see what he wanted her to do. She associated the recall sound to returning with lots of enthusiasm, but she also associated the return with three of the sounds; in fact, she had not been given the opportunity to return on one call for the handler had assumed that he needed to keep up the communication. Even issuing a 'good dog' when the dog was halfway and coming enthusiastically could have led it to believe that it had finished the action and did not need to return directly to the handler.

We humans often have a problem with keeping quiet and this is evident when I ask people to go in the training ring with my dogs and not to speak but to use body language only. Some, often the quieter or more timid handlers, are successful at this, but quite often people cannot resist making a sound of some kind, even if it is only a shushing sound to make the dog move, rather than to use a natural body movement. If they use natural body language the dog will not question them for it will understand it, but if they use a voice command the dog will immediately question them for it will not yet be used to this person's tone. An interesting experi-ment I have a lot of success with is with limiting the hearing. A dog will hear what it is focused on, so if it is focusing on chasing a rabbit you will have a problem getting it to hear you, hence the impor-tance of keeping your dog in your pack area and focused on you. If your dog is focused on you it will be listening to you, and to be focused it does not have to be looking at you; if this were the case guide dogs would be of little use if they had to look at their handlers to concentrate on guiding them. My dogs work sheep and they are looking at the sheep when they are working, but their hearing is focused on me. Human beings can, and do, hear several things at once and they tend either to focus on them or unwittingly allow the different sounds to interfere with their focus. If I ask a handler to wear some earphones with pleasant music to listen to when working my dog, the results are quite definite: he focuses on the dog, he is unaware of any outside interference and will become at one with the dog and its body language. As I deny them hearing access to the human world some of the instincts that they were not aware they had rise to the surface. You might want to try this at some time when you are training or taking your dog for a walk.

Allow your dog the chance to respond to a command or to work a situation out, for if you always assume that he is going to need a second command then he will have no need to respond the first time, will he? If he does not respond to your command and you have not repeated yourself, you can go to him and make sure that he does as you have asked, whether it is a sit, a stay or a recall. You do not need to be upset or angry, just be firm and explain what you expect from him. He must learn to listen for your voice and to what you are saying and you must learn to give a sound for him to associate with each action.

Each 'Sound' Has One Meaning

Whatever words you choose for your commands you must make sure that they are not duplicated. For example, if you say 'down' to your dog to make it lie down, you cannot say 'down' to stop it jumping up, neither can you use similar commands such as 'lie down' and 'get down'. If your dog is on the furniture and you want to tell it to get down and say the word 'down' it could lie down on the furniture and, in its own mind, be doing as it was told. Neither does it matter what word you use as long as both you and your dog know what it means, that is all that is important. There are certain commands that are used almost universally and are obvious, the down, sit and stay commands are self-explanatory, but even those are each individual's choice. A good command to stop a dog jumping on furniture or up at visitors could be 'off', but a command that I think is unbeatable and is probably one of the first words my dogs learn is 'no'. This is such a useful, 'negative', word, for whatever the dog is doing when it hears the word 'no' it stops. If my dogs are barking, jumping up, getting in or out of the car without permission, or generally about to get into some form of mischief I can forewarn them with the magic word and they have no excuse whatsoever to continue and get into trouble. It is also a word that is natural to us, for it rolls automatically off the tongue and, because we know it as a negative command in our own language, we find it natural to put on the correct emphasis.

The 'stay' command may cause problems if it is not explained properly to the

Actions speak louder than words. When dogs are used to seeing other animals as part of everyday life they become accustomed to them and to their body language. Moss, who is a natural predator, cannot believe the body language of the goat: 'So you think I'm scared of a dog?'

'Well I'm not, so give me a kiss!' Moss is even more surprised at this action.

dog; you must decide whether it is going to mean to the dog stay until you are given permission to move or stay for a few minutes and then do as you wish. Handlers often use the stay command out of context without realizing it; how many of us are guilty of saying the word 'stay' to our dogs when we are going to bed, leaving them in the car, in the house or with a friend? In these instances the dog is not going to 'stay' when we leave it in the car – it will move around, and when we say goodnight and tell it to 'stay there' it will certainly not go the whole night

Even more unusual. 'Are you a big dog or are you a sheep?' 'I'm a sheep, and if they can kiss so can we.'

without moving. We know what we mean, but do our dogs? In most cases the dogs are conditioned-trained; they know that they are going to be left for a while and are not really taking any notice of what is being said. But it is not fair to expect a dog to stay and not move as part of its training when it hears the same sound on a regular basis and does not have to take any notice of it. You need a command that your dog will understand means that it does not move until you give it permission. If you tell your dog to go to his bed and stay there, you must remember to release him from this command within a sensible period of time, if not your 'stay' will become negotiable.

Words or commands will only mean to a dog what you teach it they mean, so if you say 'Sit' twice the dog will expect to hear it twice before performing the action. If you are using 'stay' as a command that means that it must not move until told, you could use the word 'wait' for leaving your dog for a short while, but, once again, you have to explain it to your dog. A friend of mine uses 'wait' to let her dog know that it must listen as there is an important command about to follow it; in this instance I tell my dogs to 'listen'. If we were to work each other's dogs our commands would not make sense. My 'wait' command means pause, do not go on, or do not follow me. But I have two dogs who understand totally different meanings by the word and this was completely unintentional. Skye, a summer pup, was always told to wait in the yard whenever I went inside and so to her 'wait' meant 'Don't follow mum but play in the yard.' Hope, a winter pup, was told to wait in the house when I went out in the cold. Both dogs understood the general meaning and Skye never had a problem, but Hope was worried about the command when he was asked to 'wait' outside for he felt that he should be in a house and actually ran looking for shelter so that he could please me. It took far less time to re-educate him than it took to work out why he was confused in the first place. Remember Megan who always used to run very fast? I thought I was teaching her to go slower to the word 'slow' but in fact she associated the word 'slow' with a certain speed, one just slower than full gallop, it did not mean always go slower. The word meant always go slower in my language, but this was not the way she associated it to her action.

If we concentrate on sounds and syllables we can make commands that are acceptable to both our dogs and to us. Going back to not using the dog's name for each command but giving it a two-syllable command, you can roll words together and make a lovely, lyrical sound. The shepherd's recall is actually 'That will do', but rolled together the words become 'That'lldo', no pauses, sounds like one word, can be crisp or gentle and is tuneful. Stay and wait should be one syllable because the words will be used when the dog is stationary and attentive, but other commands, especially those which may be used at a distance, are better being tuneful, otherwise they may be difficult for the dog to hear clearly. Remember that when you are standing at your height your dog is very near the ground and can hear other sounds that you are not even aware of. It is then easy for a 'down', 'come' or 'stop' just to be a one-syllable blur on the wind. Other possibilities could be 'gedown', 'come't'me' or 'stopthere'. You do not have to try this but think about it, because quite often what has always seemed correct to human beings is not always easiest for the dog.

I hope this has given some food for thought and tempts you to be a little adventurous rather than sticking to what appear to be some of the more traditional commands. For some of these commands are actually of more recent years and many are born of competition training, and this type of training must not be confused with educating for good manners. They are too separate concepts; for example, in competition obedience the dog is encouraged to walk slightly in front and watching its handler. This is not the way you would go for a country walk with your dog and it will also allow your dog promotion in your pack – to your place. There is a time and place for everything, if my daughter began disco dancing around the office she would soon lose her job, and if she took her work on to the dance floor she would probably be taken to the nearest doctor! She knows how to behave at work, when to respect rules and regulations and when to enjoy free time; it is all part of education.

Actions May Be Misleading

You must always remember that body language is your dog's first language, so if it is unsure or it has not learned your language it will listen to your body. Then if you remember that it will associate a sound with an action you must make sure that unintentionally you do not give him the wrong message. For example, a new puppy may have an 'accident' on the carpet, the worst damage this can do is leave a small, wet patch, but the damage to the puppy could be irreparable if the situation is not handled with care. If the owner reads the puppy's body language and anticipates what is going to happen they will be able to show the puppy that this is not the place to be used. But if they jump forwards, using a loud voice, grabs the puppy and then puts it where they want it to go (and in the heat of the moment it is easy to do this and with all the right intentions), they will probably frighten the life out of it. The result will be a puppy who is nervous of the 'new' pack leader and is also frightened to do anything in front of them, preferring to hide each time it needs to relieve itself; it will associate a normal function with displeasing the leader. Sometimes we do not always think before we speak, but we must make an effort to think before we make an action with our body language that will send the wrong message to the dog; the big mistake in the situation just described is taking the puppy by surprise. If a puppy is surprised or frightened it needs to be to able to run to you for security, but if you are the one who upsets it, albeit unintentionally, it will try and find security elsewhere.

A dog does not necessarily see things the way we expect it to, and we must make allowances for this. The first time you take your puppy in a car you may be worried that it will be frightened of the noise of the engine or of the motion of the car and, anxious to make sure you are reassuring your dog, raise it so that it can see out of the window. This may make sense to us because the dog can see out and know that the outside world is still normal, but, as was mentioned earlier, this 'familiar' scenery is suddenly rushing backwards at a frightening speed. The dog does not see the world through our eyes so we must try and see it through his. If your dog is nervous on its first car

This view from a car window shows the scenery as we see it when the car is stationary.

This is not a mistake: this is the view taken from a car window when travelling at low speed. Remember that when the car moves it can be disorienting for a dog until it becomes used to the world moving 'backwards'.

ride and it detects a note of anxiety in your voice you will be strengthening his fears instead of reassuring him. The word association for him in this instance would need to be gentle but firm and with a happy tone, one he associates with pleasure and the expectation of good things to come. If a 'treat' is used to try and reassure the dog its mind may be taken from the worry of the car while it is eating, but when the food is finished it will either refocus on its previous fears or search frantically around for another 'treat'. At no point is the handler saying to the dog that there is nothing to fear. The very fact that the handler is trying to divert the dog's attention is enough to convince it that something is wrong and it could soon

If your dog is travelling in your car regularly, make sure that you provide plenty of ventilation, for even a short stay in a car without ventilation can be fatal for a dog. This estate car has wire doors at the rear and specially made grids for the windows and the sun roof.

begin to realize that anxiety produces titbits. Unfortunately, this may have the repercussion of the dog's not only failing to learn that there is nothing to be frightened of and that the pack leader is in control, but a clever dog can eventually use this as manipulation at a later date.

When someone knocks on the door and a dog barks, the natural reaction for the dog's owner is usually to tell it to be quiet. But does the dog know what the word quiet means? It probably does, but it will not necessarily be the meaning the owner intended it to have. There is a command in dog training called the 'speak' command and this entails the dog's 'speaking' (barking) on command; it

is not difficult to teach, for most handlers will automatically use the subliminal training method, they will encourage the dog to bark and then give the 'speak' sound. Dogs can be encouraged to bark or yap quite easily and many handlers are proud when they have this new command to use. But I have never quite understood the concept of encouraging a dog to be noisy, almost as if touching a button, without having an even quicker button available to shut it up. It is not as easy to teach 'quiet' as it is to teach 'speak' for it is not usually an issue until it is too late and the dog is already in full voice. If you read your dog's body language he will tell you when he is going to bark, so before he

If a dog is constantly kept on the go with balls and toys and not taught to be content with its own company, it will find it difficult to rest. It may create unnecessary mischief which can lead to damage; this dog is chasing the football on the television.

begins give him a firm 'no' and bring him in behind you. When he barks you tell him 'no', which is the negative command, and the second he thinks that he should not bark tell him 'quiet', in a firm but soothing tone. You can arrange this tuition just as you can arrange his good-manners training when there is a knock on the door. Always use whatever happens in everyday life in the home to your advantage; do not wait until you are out with your dog to teach him something new. There will always be a time when he commits himself to an action in the house that at the time may not bother you but that may eventually create a problem.

For example, one distressed family came to me with a problem dog that was jumping up at the window and barking at the least noise it heard outside. This dog had not suddenly begun to do this, it had been teaching itself over a period of weeks, but it had been unnoticed by its family until it had become a huge problem with the dog biting the windowsill. Among the methods they had used to try to stop the dog they had told it to be quiet, called it a good dog, shouted at it, used both toys and titbits and, in desperation, had blocked access to the window with a chair. By shouting 'quiet' to it when it was barking it understood that the word meant it had to bark, so they were actually commending its behaviour in its eyes. When the family shouted, the dog thought they were joining in and, of course, the 'good boy' toys and titbits only served to convince him that he was pleasing them. In fact, he even had to eat a chair when it got in his way to make sure that he did not let them down. If we look at the situation through the dog's eyes we see that he had learned that he could look out of the window by jumping up to the sill, he had found it great fun barking at anything that moved. This had progressed almost to imagining that he could hear something and all the time his humans were giving him plenty of attention. To begin with, the family concerned had to realize that the dog associated the word 'quiet' which they had been using with barking and, secondly, that they had to take back ownership of the room. The first step was to revert to the training method used when teaching a dog that it does not own the house, for this dog could no longer be allowed to assume that it could do as it pleased in the living room. One evening it was 'invited' into the room and made to sit in its own bed for a few moments before being allowed the freedom of the room. It could go near the window only if it behaved as its owners wanted it to; if it barked it was told to go back to its bed; if it sat quietly it was introduced to a new word for 'quiet' and told it was good. There were other factors to be taken into consideration because the dog pulled on a lead, did not have a recall and its diet needed changing. But a problem rarely stands on its own; it is always one of many other little traits of bad manners that eventually turn into a big problem. After three weeks the dog could sit in the room and be trusted not to bark nor jump up at the window. It was three weeks of hard work for the owners, not just because they were training their dog but because they had to begin to 'think' dog. They had to learn to listen to themselves so that they did not repeat their commands and they had to change certain words. The 'quiet' which the dog interpreted as an indication that it could bark became 'calm' and the 'leave' they used to make it drop a toy or ball when it was demanding, and which it ignored, became 'dropit'. They had to begin a new regime of word association.

Consistency

No amount of training, body language or the correct use of words will prove successful if you are not consistent. Little and often is the recipe for success. There is no point in being diligent with your dog one day and then allowing him to do as he pleases for the rest of the week; and there is no such thing as being too short of time. If someone really, genuinely does not have a few moments free each day to give their dog some quality time and simple education *then they should not have a dog*. We all have days when we are rushing around and maybe cannot spend the amount of time we would like to spend with them. Nevertheless, all dogs, large or small, are living beings and if we take them into our lives and our homes then we owe them some quality of life and this means both education and those special bonding moments. It does not mean that every day a dog must have so many miles of exercise and a certain amount of training, quite the contrary, for a walk that does not involve companionship is not beneficial to a dog, and neither is training for half an hour and then nothing for a couple of weeks. At some point in each day we will take time, it may be for a drink, a sit down, reading a paper or watching television. Each of these situations can be shared with a dog, and in so doing the dog can be taught good manners in many of the ways we have already discussed. You must be consistent and your dog must know where he stands with you or he will endeavour to create a role of his own making, and you won't be the pack leader.

Dogs can communicate with movements of their bodies, so if we are to communicate with them in their own language, in order to enable us to teach them our language, then we must learn to give the kinds of movement they will recognize. Dogs will mimic each other; this is how they learn, so we must give them something sensible to mimic. If you are boisterous with your dog he will think that this is the way he should behave; if you have a small or timid dog who has not a naturally boisterous character he may feel threatened or overpowered. However, if you have a dominant or very energetic dog he will soon be jumping up and returning your body language with great enthusiasm, and if you are not careful he may just be treating everyone he meets with the same kind of energetic 'play'. If you wave your arms in the air and use a high-pitched voice he will see it as overenthusiasm and will become excited. This is the kind of movement he would associate with play and with a litter-mate. If you use exaggerated arm movements which are sharp and strong he will see this as 'shouting' and if you add a loud voice he could interpret it as aggression. If you want your dog to remain calm and sensible, and this is the only way he can really learn, then your language must be calm and sensible too and this means your body language. Word association does not only apply to voice commands but also to the language he will recognize first, body language. Consistency is just as important with your body language, for no matter what you may be saying with your voice, until he understands every word without any hesitation it is your body language he will be reading. If you are trying to convince him with your voice that you are the pack leader and you can protect him but your body is bent over and appears vulnerable, then he will not be reassured by your voice for your body will be telling him a different story. If you are telling him he is a good lad while all the time you are waving your arms in the air or playing with his lead or a toy he will listen to your body and decide that you are playing a game. If you are trying to tell him he has just done a marvelous training session, he will have forgotten all about it and will be focusing on fun. This is all very well, but if he has just deserved a commendation from you then he should know exactly what it is for in order for him to do it again. Face your dog and smile – dogs love a smile, it is a relaxed expression and is the opposite of a snarl and, yes, they can mimic it if not with their mouth then with their eyes, then tell him he is a good lad. Stroke him in preference to patting him for it is gentler, and let him be quiet for a moment; then, if you wish, you can both share a jump for joy. This way your dog is reading your body language, which is quiet, and you are giving him a moment to think about what he has just accomplished and how it pleased you. Any play you may engage in afterwards then is a 'treat' and not part of the reason for being called a 'good lad'.

If you speak loudly to your dog he will reciprocate with 'loud' body actions for he will move faster and often without thinking about his actions. If you whisper he will use softer actions and he will also have to stay focused in order to hear you. Never train in a loud voice, dogs have wonderful hearing and can hear you when they are at quite a distance, but if you do not educate them to keep listening to you they will soon focus on something else.

How Should We Chastise?

Theoretically, if we do everything right our dogs will not make mistakes, but would it not be boring? A good dog needs to question, for just like a child it cannot learn if it does not ask, and there will be times when it feels it has to challenge the boundaries you have set it. It would not be a living being if it did not try to keep stretching itself, and as long as it tests the boundaries and does not step over them it will not be breaking any rules. Much will depend on how well you have taught your dog always to be aware of you and on how well you have learned to read your dog. If you are taking no notice when the young dog reaches a boundary (mental or physical) then it must commit itself to breaking a rule. Children will often test their parents' commitment to rules by threatening to break them, but they are not really expecting to get away with it and, if they do, they often cannot handle any situation which may arise from their insubordination. Young dogs are no different, a pup will try and trick its mother and expect her to tell him off. The young dog will test the superiors in the pack and expect to be put in his place; it is all part of growing up. Do not see it as

the young trying to break the rules, more the young making sure that you are committed to keeping them.

But what if a dog really does break a rule? In the first place we have to admit that we are at fault; there is no such thing as a bad dog, human beings must bear the responsibility. Very few dogs are born bad and if they are it is a direct result of bad breeding; we can hardly blame the dog for that when humans are responsible for the mating in the first place. If a puppy makes mistakes it is up to the owner to correct it as soon as possible or, better still, try to prevent bad habits from forming by teaching a solid foundation of good manners. If an older dog makes mistakes then a refresher course in good manners or even the building of a new foundation may be necessary, but in each instance it is an owner or previous owner who has made mistakes. Bearing this in mind, it would seem wrong to punish a dog for something we probably encouraged or allowed it to do in the first place; however, a dog, like a child, cannot be allowed to keep breaking rules.

Scruffing

'Scruffing' – taking hold of the hair on a dog's neck and shaking the dog – is not an action I advise, for each dog will interpret the action in a different way. Some will be frightened or nervous when they are scruffed and this can make them submissive. Some will see it as an act of aggression and react with a growl; some may even turn on the person scruffing them. The theory behind scruffing is that the pack leader would stand over an insubordinate and shake it; there is also an assumption that the dominant dog would be growling, so the handler will often imitate a deep growl when chastising his dog in this manner. I cannot deny that a dominant dog will behave in such a manner, but are you a dominant dog or pack leader? The pack leader must not be seen as having to resort to violence each time a dog steps out of line; if he is a good leader he will not have allowed it to happen. If such an occasion arises he is not admonishing the dog so much as he is protecting his own role as leader and therefore he will be far more concerned about being the winner than about the other dog's reaction. He will be standing over the dog and growling and he will have every intention of carrying the commitment to this threat through by fighting; this could lead to a fight to the death or to the loser being cast from the pack. The rules are the same throughout the animal kingdom, including our own. The punishment must fit the crime, but if your dog's crime does not fit the punishment you are in trouble. Was it really such a bad one that you are going to fight him and eventually cast him out? If you use this method, whatever the outcome you will lose, for the result may not be desirable. If the dog is made submissive, you have lost a very important part of its character. If your dog returns the aggression it could bite you, causing another problem larger than the first. If you lose the fight, you are hurt and your dog has succeeded in being the 'boss', if you win the fight what have you gained? For you have not taught your dog that he should not bite because you instigated the aggression in the first place. Whatever the outcome your dog will still be in your pack and so your show of 'violence' was

Body language can tell a story. The dog is advancing on the cat, his body is tense and the cat is almost mirroring this tenseness.

When the cat turns away, the dog relaxes his body, confident that he is in control but waiting to see what the cat's next move is.

When the cat moved away, the dog tried to stop it but the cat confronted him. The dog must now decide whether to fight (which he knows he should not do) or to be submissive to a cat. Either way he would take a pounding with the cat's claws or dented pride. Fortunately for him, he was given a recall and this saved him from any embarrassment. This is a similar situation to the confrontation of a dog walking on a path with its handler and being faced with an oncoming 'threat'.

not carried through to casting him out, so he now can see a weakness in your rules. Never have a confrontation with a dog. Whatever the outcome you will not win, strive to be a true leader ruling through respect.

I have been told of various forms of chastisement used on dogs, ranging from rolled-up newspapers, water squirters, pinching their ears and sulking with them, to locking them outside or in a shed. Many are then introduced to another variety of treat almost like a pleasure/pain theory: when they are wrong they are punished, when they are right they get a treat, ranging from bits of liver, sweets, toys, fancy gadgets to things that go click or make other noises. If parents used all or even some of these methods on their children there would be an outcry from onlookers. You teach a child the difference between right and wrong, then if it should step out of line you can explain that it must not happen again. If it does something you think deserves recognition it gets a treat, but everyday good manners are expected and do not warrant a great shower of sweets each time they are displayed. There is no substitute in dog training and the education of good manners for communication, and if you learn the language of your dog and then teach him your language you will be building a relationship that is akin to that of parent and child. You will know your dog and you will know what is the best way to handle good and bad behaviour. The tone of your voice will tell him when he is right or wrong and, if you use your voice correctly and with a lyrical sound when necessary, you will not need any other form of 'sound' communication. Clicks, rattles, squeaks or whatever is in fashion (and these training aids have

not been around for ever, but well-behaved dogs have) are not sounds your dog would expect to hear, so if you are going to use them do it only for extra training. If you are training for a special kind of discipline your trainer may request that you try one of the special aids; this is entirely up to you but for basic good manners and a sensible, well-trained pet dog you do not need anything other than yourself and a good dose of common sense.

Dealing with Bad Manners in the Home

The concept of the pack leader standing over the insubordinate is correct, but you are not a dog, you are human and must not put yourself into a position of weakness or one where you cannot follow through like a dog. If your dog misbehaves in your house then he must be made to stay in his own (his bed) to think about his behaviour and with no toys or bones. This does not make his bed a place of punishment, it makes it a place where he can sit and think. The rule is straightforward, if you cannot behave in my house with my rules then you must go and sit in your own until told otherwise, and you cannot borrow any of my possessions (toys) until you are worthy of this privilege.

Dealing with Bad Manners Outside

Bad manners or bad behaviour outside the home pack area can be manifested in many ways. We have dealt with the recall, walking in the pack area and keeping

Bad manners in the home are not acceptable. You may know your dog is friendly but do not expect your visitors to feel the same way; a big dog can be frightening when it jumps up. When a dog has let you know there is someone at the door he should be content to let you deal with the matter, unless you give him permission to do otherwise.

have a dog that does not yet fully understand his place in the pack then it is better not to take him into an area where he may misbehave until you have either built or rebuilt his foundation of good manners. However, if dogs did not take us by surprise, training would be unbelievably easy, so if your dog does take matters into his own hands – and it is usually with a show of aggression to other dogs or people – bring him into your pack area and make him lie down. Do not try to push an aggressive dog down and do not try to out-stare one, either may result in your getting bitten. Make sure you stand between your dog and the object of its focus. If he shows aggression when you are going for a walk and you are able to make him walk behind you, then try to continue with your walk, ignore him and keep your body relaxed. But if at any time he tries to push in front of you then bring him back into your space and make him lie down.

If your dog is aggressive and you are not able to control it then you must seek professional help. Each case of aggression is dependent on many different factors and therefore cannot be solved without both the dog and the handler being seen by the person who is giving advice.

I have heard of owners being told to ignore their dogs when they jump up at them after being on their own for a while and being told to sulk with their dogs. I have to say that I could never have ignored my children when they were pleased to see me and neither could I my dogs. But I can say a great big 'Hello' to them and then ask them to go to their beds while I put the kettle on and sit down, and then we can have a hug. Do not confuse thinking time with sulking. Sulking is resorting to non-pack

behind. If these have been applied correctly then your dog will not embarrass you, for he will not make decisions without checking with you first. If you behaviour, but thinking time is when the dog has not strived to please and therefore must spend some time thinking about his actions. You are not sulking with him, you are telling him to be quiet and not to disturb you while he thinks about his actions.

Learn to interpret your dog's intentions and you will be able to prevent problems from arising; use your tone of voice to let him know how you feel and make sure your dog can relate the sound you choose to the action you want. When you have your dog's good manners under control and you have taught him your language, it is time to look at some everyday occurrences and how they may affect your dog.

Chapter Summary

If you teach your dog to focus on you and to listen to you it will respond to your commands at a distance and even if it cannot see you. Do not repeat your commands and do not use titbits or treats to try and gain your dog's respect. Learn to train subliminally, teaching your dog the word you want him to understand for an action, when he is actually thinking of performing that action.

CHAPTER 9

The Way We See It

Without realizing it, we are often guilty of inflicting our opinions on our dogs. We decide what they like and how they like it, but quite often, were they given a choice, things would be different. We have to be in control and obviously there are certain times when, whatever the dog wants, 'human must rule, OK'. But for the very reason that we make sure the dog does as we say in important areas, we should allow it the chance to do a little decision-making for itself in areas of lesser importance.

Does a dog really have a favourite toy or do we think it has? Most dogs will favour one particular toy, but did the dog choose it or did we? Quite often a dog will find himself something to play with, it could be a toy, a piece of wood or any other natural substance. He will be content with this, but we are the masters of interference, we just have to take it from him and introduce something 'better'. If the something 'better' is readily accepted we assume that he was bored with the toy of his own choosing. If the dog is not really enthusiastic we set about showing him all the good games he could be missing by not giving the new toy a chance. If we jump up and down long enough and keep him amused, he will eventually play with the toy just so that he can see us go through our paces. This is, of course, a humorous account, but it quite easily could be true and is, in fact, true in part. For we do tend

to keep introducing new objects and ideas to our dogs, but quite often they are not ready for them and in some cases do not even need them.

A dog will often appear to favour one particular walk, but is it the dog's favourite walk or does its owner happen to like it? Dogs aim to please and they are susceptible to our moods so that when we are happy or sad we unwittingly transmit our feelings to them. If we prefer one particular walk we will be in a lighter, more carefree and happier mood while we are walking. Our dogs will be aware of this feeling of well-being and, because we are more relaxed and more communicative, they will benefit from it. Therefore our dogs will enjoy the walk and will learn to associate it with pleasure and will appear to favour it. Of course, the dog may prefer that particular walk, but which came first? Do we prefer the walk because we think the dog likes it, or does the dog prefer the walk because we like it and are happier then? The answer in this instance is irrelevant, both dog and owner are happy and no harm is being done, but there are some instances when we need to be certain that we are not making our dog's decisions for him, and sometimes we must 'wean' the dog from his preferences.

If a dog decides that its favourite toy is something that makes an irritating sound the owner would try and guide it to another less noisy toy; but who gave it the toy in the first place? The owner sees a toy, decides that their dog would like it, encourages it to play with it, but if it becomes annoying will then tell the dog it must find another one.

Nearly all dog owners at some time will encourage their dog to retrieve; it may be to fetch a ball, the post, a newspaper or anything that the dog can safely carry in its mouth. Some dogs are natural retrievers and will happily comply, some are just not interested and some get so carried away with the idea that they are on a constant mission to keep the 'boss' supplied with a stream of goodies. But it is not a statutory requirement for every dog to be able to bring a ball back whenever its owner feels like throwing it away. If you want to teach your dog to retrieve,

and it is willing to learn, then let this be a bonus rather than an essential requirement. When your dog has perfected the art you will be able to enjoy a game of 'I'll throw it and you fetch it', but it is only a game, it is not a means of getting your dog back to you, and remember that games can be played to excess. What a human may see as a dog having fun may actually be a dog getting so wound up that it is not thinking straight.

Barking

Dogs will usually have a reason for barking. If they are frightened they may bark to try and ward off a possible attacker; if they are aggressive they will

Dogs usually have a reason for barking: Di has seen someone in her yard and is not happy about it.

She is making sure that everyone knows there is a stranger about.

Her body is beginning to relax as she hands authority over to the 'boss', but she is still not sure.

bark with dominance; and they will bark a warning to protect their 'pack'. Different kinds of bark will be used for different meanings and some breeds are more vocal than others; but when dogs are playing with each other in the wild they rarely bark. A bark usually carries a message but yapping is high-pitched and quite often the result of excitement, and this can be induced when owners play with their dogs. It is a misguided conception that a dog must be making a lot of noise to enjoy itself and if we study the body language we can see why. If a dog is yapping its body movements will be jerky, its tail will be waving wildly in the air and it will not be focusing on anything. When a dog becomes excited during a game to the point of high-pitched yapping it is usually bordering on hysteria. This is not doing it any good, for it will not tire it out: it may exhaust it for a short while but then it will bounce back for more. This does not mean that it is wrong for your dog to be barking, but do think about the way it is doing it and what induced it, for if we ran around shouting all the time we would be classed as hooligans. Small doses of barking may be acceptable, but if your dog is going to turn into a hooligan then make him rethink the game.

Working and Playing

Dog training is fun and if you teach your dog by playing games it will enjoy its education, but you have to differentiate between training for basic obedience and teaching your dog something extra. Basic obedience and good manners are essential and must be taken seriously; your dog must learn them to become a respectable, well-mannered, go-anywhere creature. Any other training is an extra, it is something that is not absolutely necessary but would be valuable if your dog learned it, this includes training for the disciplines.

It is not essential that a dog can accomplish a first-class retrieve, do the weaving poles in record time and excel at 'scent', yet it is not unusual for a dog to have all these abilities and be thoroughly bad-mannered. We teach children by play, but we also make sure that they remain focused and that they do learn from the game. We are actually grooming them for work. They begin with the pre-school level then to infant, then junior, and when they attend secondary school they are being taught to work, and play is something they do outside school hours. When they leave school they are accustomed to the fact that there is a time for work and

Dogs are full of fun and love freedom of movement. Kim is enjoying the thrill of jumping over a very fine chicken mesh, which she still jumps over after it has been moved.

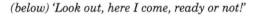

a time for play. We want our children to be sensible members of society and with a sense of responsibility. Yet quite often dogs are so play-oriented that they have no concept of work. Work does not apply just to working dogs, it means teaching a dog that not everything is a game, for if it were there would be no sense of urgency – everything would be play and a recall would not be important. We all know that the recall is important and so we teach our dogs that this is not a game. Yes, we teach it in a pleasurable way, but the dog must show commitment to obedience and to the pack leader, it must work at getting it right so that it can earn the right to play.

I once received a letter from someone who was concerned about the attitude of a

(above) Up and over.

(below) 'Look out, here I come, ready or not!'

Make sure that your dog has regular access to water, especially if it is spending time outside in the garden.

dog handler whom she had seen at a competition. Her worry was that the dogs were kept in cages in a car, and, when she had moved to go towards them, had been asked by the owner to leave them alone as they were 'due to work'. The writer of the letter was disgusted that the dogs were caged and were being kept for 'work' when they should have been enjoying life. She also pointed out that most of the dogs at the competition were barking and running round wagging their tails and obviously enjoying themselves. As I was not in attendance at this show I do not know whether the handler in question was, in fact, showing disregard for the dogs, but I do know that dogs love to work. Like children, they enjoy being given a task to excel at, and, if they are to do it to the best of their ability, they need to concentrate. Dogs running around, barking and flying their tails are not concentrating and they are rarely focusing on their handlers. It is quite probable that the handler in question was being sensible, was keeping her dogs quiet and was protecting their space, which the letter-writer had no right to invade. It was also equally possible that when they were at home those dogs had as much if not more fun than some of the others. A little knowledge can be a dangerous thing, and the writer of the letter took what she saw at face value and

A dog well-educated but not stimulated to the point of overexcitement will be quite content to enjoy free time chewing a bone.

actually knew very little about dogs and their welfare, never having owned one. It is essential to do what is right for you and your dog and not to be ruled by opinion, for it is you who will have to live with the consequences if you commit yourself to something you feel to be wrong.

There is a fine line between being too play-oriented and too committed to work; training must have some flexibility for you are dealing with a living being. If you are not sure how your dog will respond to certain methods then take some time to study him, for when you know him, how he thinks and reacts to certain situations you will automatically know how to educate him. When to work and when to play will then come naturally to you, but always make sure that you introduce variety into his education and into each day.

Work Time

This can be education for good manners and basic training. It can be a one-to-one training session for competition work or it can be more advanced training for just you and your dog to learn new things together.

Playtime

This is not necessarily a 'chase around and have a silly half-hour time', it is time for handler and dog to enjoy some

Or just relaxing in a shady spot.

time interacting with each other without a toy or any kind of aid, just learning about each other's skills in a relaxed way.

Playtime with a Toy

If your dog plays with toys and enjoys them then let him have a 'treat' time when he can play and enjoy himself by devising his own games, join in with him and you can both have fun, but keep the games sensible and try to 'listen' to what he wants.

Three Essential Rules of Time

Free time, thinking time and quality time: every dog deserves time to itself, doing whatever it enjoys, in its own space and undisturbed by humans – free time to be a dog. Thinking time is greatly underestimated by many owners but it is essential for all dogs. A time when they are not being constantly told what to do and how to do it, but neither are they supplied with toys or things to do to keep them amused. They must learn to be patient, to enjoy their own company and to work things out. Quality time is probably the most important time of all; this is when you share moments together that do not include other humans or dogs; a time for you to learn about each other, to understand each other, to bond and to create a wonderful empathy with each other. Quality time takes the ownership out of the human–dog relationship and creates a partnership.

How Important Is Diet?

Your dog's diet is very important, and not just because he needs to eat but because he needs to eat a good, sensible diet that complements both his breed and his lifestyle. If you are starting out with a puppy you will probably have been recommended a particular brand of food by the breeder and, whatever preference you may have, it would not be wise to change the diet too quickly. The breeder should have a knowledge of what food is best for their line of dog; but not all breeders will see the results of the diet if they do not take a puppy through to maturity. Some breeders will have come to an arrangement with a pet food company or a local store; nutrition is not to be taken lightly and each breed will have individual requirements. When you choose your breed talk to breed specialists and discuss feeding with them. I say specialists in the plural for they all have their own ideas and reasons for particular diets. For example, if your dog is a working breed, spaniel, retriever or Border Collie, for example, it will have a naturally high energy level and, as an adult, it will not need to be fed 'energy fuel'. If you were to ask the advice of someone who competes with their dog and it uses up a large amount of energy he may recommend a food which is suitable for his dog's energy level but could be totally unsuitable for yours. If you feed an energy food to a dog that is not utilizing it correctly it could become hyperactive. So make sure that when you seek advice that it is for *your* dog and not just the breed in general.

Also remember that manufacturers of dog food cannot possible give advice for every breed of dog on their packaging, they can only give guidelines. Large dogs such as St Bernards or Newfoundlands will still be growing when they are over one year old and will therefore need food that caters for this growth rate. Medium-sized breeds, such as Springer Spaniels or Border Collies, will not have a high growth rate from six months onwards. Small breeds, some of the terriers and toys will reach their full size when they are still very young. So always take size and the growth rate into consideration and study the temperament of your chosen breed. If you have a breed that is recognized for being full of energy or dominant then you must make sure that you are not giving it too much energy, but a breed of a more docile nature or a slower metabolism may need a more energy-giving diet.

Now you need to study your own lifestyle and the time of the year; if you are giving your dog plenty of exercise you may not notice a build up of hidden energy caused by diet. If that exercise is suddenly reduced and the dog's diet is not changed you may find that it begins to act out of character through having surplus, unexpended energy which will be causing it great frustration. For example, in summer many dogs will spend more time in the garden, it does not get dark so early in the evening and so the walks are longer, holidays and days out often entail more walking and there are clubs and competitions to enter. In winter the nights are darker, the walks are often shorter, the garden is out of bounds or the weather is wet and weekends are spent at home. If you have an energetic dog and you know he will be going through a period of reduced exercise, do not wait until he is biting his fingernails or has driven you mad with his restlessness.

Alter his diet! If you do not understand the energy levels set out on the packaging remember a few guidelines: meat is energy-giving so a high meat content means higher energy. Colourants may cause a dog to be hyperactive. Milk and eggs are high in protein and therefore high energy, so cut out any morning cereal and dish of milk for a full-grown dog. Red meat is higher energy-giving than white and vegetable protein is lower in energy than meat protein. Whether you feed tinned food, fresh food or dry 'complete' food is your choice, but if your dog's behaviour suddenly becomes questionable and you know that it is not because of lack of education then do look to his diet. If you are contemplating feeding your dog 'naturally', as you think he would be fed in the wild, bear in mind that 'natural' meat would have been killed and eaten fresh, not fresh from the butchers. Herbage would not be subject to pollution and he would be free to roam over a wide area for his hunting and grazing. It would be extremely difficult to feed your dog completely naturally, and so do not feel guilty if you are feeding something prepared by human hands as long as it is good food and meets your dog's requirements.

Do dogs become bored with food or is this just the way we see it? In the wild a dog will kill and eat both meat and bones, then between meat meals it will graze on vegetation – you could say it is used to 'meat and two veg'. Before fast food overcame us, we had a similar kind of diet and quite often families would have certain meals on particular days of the week. As we have become accustomed to a more varied diet so have our tastes changed and now many people will find the original staple diet bland, having developed a taste for unusual or novel foods. You do need to find a food for your dog that he likes and that is good for him; but if you keep changing the food he will become accustomed to expect a change. There will be necessary changes, such as from puppy food to adult food, and there may be times when the diet must be changed for the sake of a dog's health, for example, having allergies or being overweight. I have yet to meet a dog bored with its food; however, I have met many owners who have been convinced that their dog was bored with its food. It usually follows a pattern, for not all dogs have the same feeding requirements, some are greedy and some eat only what their body needs. It is not unusual for a dog suddenly to turn its nose up at its food, thus causing its owner distress. Is it poorly, is it unhappy or is it bored with its food? If it is obviously neither of the first two the conclusion is drawn that the dog is in need of a change of diet; it is then introduced to a 'new menu' and within a few weeks the pattern repeats itself.

In the wild a predator will kill and eat its fill, then it will rest; dogs will usually take a day before they begin nibbling again. So the dog that appears to be bored with its food is often simply resting its digestive system. As long as there is no medical reason for it to be refusing to eat, it is usually wiser to respect its decision to 'fast', for this is nature's way for the dog to keep healthy. If you offer him a change of food you will more than likely look for something 'special' and he will be tempted to eat it. If a child leaves their vegetables, claiming that they are too full to eat them, they will no doubt still find room for a piece of chocolate. Once a dog realizes that it can hold you to ransom over his food he will continue to appear 'bored', and each time you change the food you are, in effect, extending his choice. In addition, he is not getting the staple diet his body requires. Without realizing it, you have begun to educate him to demand a change in his menu and eventually you will run out of ideas for variety.

I often have people coming to me because they are concerned about their dog's behaviour and one of the first areas I question will be diet. It will have been changed many times and the owner is usually quite desperate as to how to keep varying it, so meat has been added to complete food, eggs to cereal and so on, until the dog is no longer getting a sensible, balanced diet. When I insist that the dog is put on one brand of food and is not offered a choice the owner is often convinced that the dog will starve, but it has not happened yet and all those fussy eaters soon learn to lick the dish clean. I am aware that some dogs are genuinely not interested in food; I live with one and she can look at her food sometimes as if I had just dug it up from the garbage pile. I have never made a fuss of her eating habits, but I did give plenty of thought to her diet when she was younger, and because she ate very little I gave her a slightly higher (and only slightly) energy content than the other dogs. At the time of writing she is fourteen years old and in lovely condition; she still thinks food is a waste of time; she has not been educated to keep changing diet; she is fit and healthy and does not look her age. So before you give in to a human interpretation make sure that you are not misreading your dog's natural digestive requirements.

When Should I Feed My Dog?

A puppy will need feeding little and often, but as it grows its need for extra food will diminish and by the time it reaches adulthood it should need only one feed a day. It is up to you how you feed your dog, and some owners do give adult dogs an extra feed in the morning, but quite often it is the habit of the owner and not the dog that is being nurtured. If a dog does not get the morning feed it will not sit all day wondering why and it will soon break the habit of expecting it, especially if it is not allowed to go to the feeding area, as this would trigger off the memory of breakfast. What and how you feed will often depend on the breed of dog; a big dog has a big appetite and so it would be advisable to select a sensible food that will satisfy him and meet his requirements without being too expensive. Small dogs do not eat as much as big ones and therefore a more luxurious diet will not be too expensive. Dogs with long hair on their faces, especially around their mouths, will be very messy if they are fed soft or runny food, so try to keep to food with a firm texture. Whatever you choose make sure that you are thinking ahead and to what his requirements will be when he is fully grown so that you can cater for his varying energy needs.

I never advise too much routine when feeding. Your dog should have his meal at roughly the same time each day; but if you make it exactly the same time and if you follow a certain routine you will find that you will not be able to vary this without your dog complaining. My dogs are fed in the morning but I do not have a set time; if I did they would begin 'asking' and then 'demanding' their food, not just

Give your dogs privacy when they are eating by feeding them in separate areas. It may be in their beds, cages or just a distance apart. These dogs are in separate rooms and the door could be closed on them. This is not a question of pecking order or of dominance, it is simply giving privacy and allowing them to eat at their own pace.

at that time but slightly before it. Try to keep a more flexible routine and you will not become a slave to a timetable. Your dog should have a place of his own to eat, where he knows that he will not be disturbed; allow him time to eat his meal and then remove the dish. If he does not eat all his food do not leave it for him to come back to later: for the sake of his digestion and your peace of mind he must learn to eat when the food is provided.

It doesn't make any difference to your dog when he eats, and it will not make him better behaved or you a pack leader if you make him wait until after you have eaten. Although the pack leader would expect to eat first, it would be taking its fill of a fresh kill before allowing the rest of the pack to eat. You are not eating a raw, freshly-killed piece of meat out in the field and your dog is not sitting at the table in a 'bib and tucker', so your meal and his are separate entities. I never put a theory forward on paper alone, I always make sure that I can prove it, and I have lost count of the number of owners who have come to me with a problem concerning a badly-behaved dog that has always been fed after them. To gain your dog's respect and to be a pack leader you have to look at the picture through his, not human, eyes.

Aggression

What is aggression? According to the dictionary, to be aggressive means to make attacks, be forceful and self-assertive. Many human beings show this kind of behaviour and most, if not all of us, are capable of it should the situation demand such a reaction. This does not mean that we go around fighting every other human we see, nor do we bite the postman and the milkman. Aggression is a natural part of any animal; it is how it is harnessed and how it is controlled that is important. If a child is allowed to use aggressive behaviour and this gets results, then it is quite possible that the child will grow up to be a bully. A dog has a natural survival instinct that tells it that there is a need to protect itself, but when it is part of a pack the leader makes the decisions and he will tell the pack whether or not it can react to certain situations.

Aggression can manifest itself in many forms and often it has become serious before the handler realizes this and then seeks help. There are two places in a pack, the leader and the pack itself: if a dog is a natural pack leader he will want to make decisions; if he has not been educated with good manners and basic obedience he will be in front making those decisions. When he sees another dog and

Dogs have an indomitable spirit that provides them with wonderful characters; if this spirit is not nurtured correctly a dog can become aggressive or submissive. Tetley is tiptoeing on to his boundary fence.

He is now in position to see everyone who passes.

He could be nice; he could be naughty. If Tetley continues to do this he will eventually stop sneaking and take it as his right to guard the fence; this little misdemeanour needs correcting before he goes on permanent path patrol.

decides that he does not like it, he becomes hostile towards the dog. If the other retreats 'Mr Macho' has won; if the other dog stands his ground 'Mr Macho' has a fight on his paws and, win or lose, his owner has a problem.

If a dog is not a natural pack leader it may be nervous or sensitive, and, if its owner does not offer it the protection that it needs by being a leader, the dog may feel threatened and vulnerable when it sees another dog. This kind of dog will not feel that it can retreat to its owner and so may give a nervous growl to ward off a possible intruder. If the growl provokes aggression from another dog there may be a fight and the nervous dog will not only be frightened of other dogs but it will no longer trust its owner for allowing it to happen in the first place. Should it win the fight or should the other dog ignore it, then it will feel that the only way forward is to keep displaying nervous aggression.

Some dogs may not feel as threatened by their own kind but show aggression to people; their behaviour pattern will be exactly the same as it would be towards a dog but is usually more distressing for the owners.

When you get your dog it already has aggressive potential and you must remember this in order to be able to control it. The word aggression conjures up an unpleasant picture and so I prefer to use a different term for the embryo stage of this instinct: I think of it more as indomitable spirit. There are many true stories of dogs performing amazing feats of endurance, it could be a shepherd's dog on the mountains or a dog involved in search and rescue; but these are dogs with indomitable spirit, they had the determination and will-power to go on against all odds. Do not try to take this

away from your dog for this is what makes him special. This wonderful part of the animal psyche is not aggressive, but if it is not understood then a dog may become aggressive in order to protect its own private space. So protect your dog's spirit and individuality by allowing it to develop, but it must be developed within your pack area; your dog must not make decisions without your consent, but you must provide him with protection.

If you have established yourself as pack leader in the first few weeks your dog will know he must not make decisions, and if you have kept him inside your pack space when out on a walk the situation should not arise. If your dog is a contender for leadership always make sure that you are between him and whatever he is planning to be hostile to, and you must learn to watch the body language. Let us look at some possible scenes.

- If you are walking down a path towards an on-coming dog and you think your dog will react adversely, your body language will transmit a message to him, and he will think you are nervous of the dog.

  If you tighten your grip on the lead, tell your dog he is a good dog or stiffen your body, you will be telling your dog that you are nervous.

  If your dog pricks his ears, stiffens his body, pulls in front and raises his hackles, he is telling you he is taking control.

- If someone is approaching who is nervous of dogs their body language will transmit the fact that they are frightened and your dog's reaction could be fear or aggression.

- If someone is approaching who likes dogs to the extent of looking straight at your dog and pushing into his space uninvited, the animal could react with fear or aggression.

In each of these scenes you can prevent the dog from taking control or being frightened. Keep your own body relaxed, do not tense on the lead but talk to him with a firm voice. Do not wait until his body tells you that he is taking control or until someone has frightened him, tell him that he must go behind you – this puts him in his place if he is dominant and offers protection if he is nervous. Never tell your dog that he is a good dog when he is thinking bad thoughts: by word association you will be endorsing bad behaviour. Never succumb to shouting at your dog or tugging at his collar, for he will see you as a member of his pack joining in with the growling and fighting. If it is possible to keep him behind you and to keep walking as if nothing were happening, then he will learn to ignore other dogs and people. If it is not possible to keep moving then bring him behind you and make him lie down, do not let him stare at the other dog or person and, as soon as possible, continue on your walk; only then can you tell him he is good.

Sometimes a dog may react adversely through no fault of its own or of its handlers but through the reaction of a third party, and it is usually with dogs of a larger breed. People are often wary of big dogs, and yet many are complete softies, but when walking down a narrow pavement and faced with a dog as big as a lion many people will automatically stiffen. If the dog reacts in a similar manner, the approaching person will tense up further and the dog could then react with a growl. He has not really done

Jane and Eric share some quality time together. Big dogs can be alarming when they are barking, but many of them are just big softies.

anything wrong in his eyes for both he and the human had a 'conversation', but only he was aware of it. A smaller dog may not even be noticed by an approaching human and, if it is, they will probably have a relaxed body language and the dog will reciprocate with a friendly 'chat'; once again the person involved may not know that they were 'speaking'. Inside the body of each dog, be it large or small, is a dog's mind and instincts, we need to understand them and then be one jump in front of them to make sure that we do prevent rather than have to find a cure.

Dogs and Children

People often have strong opinions on dogs and children being under the same roof and they usually fall into two categories: dogs and children do, or do not, mix well. For myself, I believe that well-mannered, sensible dogs and children not only mix well but also learn from one another. There are two golden rules: children must be taught to understand and respect the dog, and the dog must not be hierarchy to or on the same status level as the children.

The Parents' Role

The onus lies entirely with parents and it is easy to overlook some early events that can lead to problems later. Dogs are not toys or teddy bears and children must never be allowed to see them as such; they are living beings and they are members of your family and thus your children must give them respect. Your dog must have its bed in a 'safe area', which is out of bounds to small children, and the children must have a dog-free area to play in. If your dog knows there is an area in your house and garden where it is not allowed uninvited, there will never be the risk of its stealing toys or food or of nipping, and this goes for both dogs and children.

Your dog must know that it is lower in rank than your children, so do not ignore or see amusement in your child's trying to tell your dog to 'sit' to no avail. Your dog must learn to take notice of all senior members, so make sure that he learns to respect your child's voice and that he does as he is told. Children love responsibility so encourage them to help in the upbringing and education of your dog and do not underestimate their powers of perception, for they may understand him better than you think. *Never* allow small children and dogs together unsupervised for neither can be trusted completely, they are both subject to moods and tiredness. You *must* make sure that your dog understands that your children are above him and that they are not litter mates; this is one of the biggest downfalls for dogs and children living together. Dogs are not playmates for children; they are dogs and if they see children as litter mates then they will see no wrong in following the litter mate games into nipping, as they fight for supremacy of the litter. What you will see as aggression and your dog's turning on your child will simply have been a natural reaction for your dog, but once bitten, twice shy and prevention is better than cure.

We are witness to dogs, children and mild hysteria regularly. Wherever we see balls, frisbees and running, chasing games involving children and dogs making lots of noise, there is often an accident waiting to happen. It may be when the dog is young; it may be when it is older and not as patient. It is not even necessarily within your own family, for a dog used to playing with children may approach the wrong child and frighten it, and children that are used to hugging and playing with dogs may approach a dog that is not used to children. The outcome can be disastrous but could be avoided if children are taught to respect all dogs and dogs are not allowed to see children as playmates.

Encourage children to play mind games with dogs – hide the ball, and so on – but keep the games quiet so that both dog and child are learning to interact with each other; a child will usually enjoy learning interaction of body language. A dog grows

Children love responsibility and they should be encouraged to help in training. Parents must make sure that their dog sees children as members of the hierarchy and not as litter mates. Claire enjoys teaching Benji and Benji respects her as a senior pack member; they can have fun but Claire is in control.

toddler is five years old the puppy will be a big, strong, adolescent dog. The whole picture will have changed. Small dogs will not overpower a child with their strength but their teeth can still do damage and parents usually steer clear of very large dogs. Medium-sized dogs are usually a family's choice: big enough for the children to play with but not too big or strong, and often of a working breed, they will be nimble, energetic and have a lively brain, but they are not childminders, they are dogs. If you are not used to a breed or you are a first-time dog owner and you have children, then think carefully before you get a dog. Can you cope with the extra commitment and is the breed you are thinking of suitable for your present circumstances? Your commitment to your dog should be the same as to your child, a commitment for life. If sensible education is implemented from the start a child and a dog can share some wonderful moments together, but this is dependent on parental guidance and good pack leadership.

When you have educated your dog, you are satisfied that both his manners and his obedience will not let you down and that you are the pack leader, you are ready to begin the business of living with your dog and having some serious fun.

faster than a child does, at three months old a puppy may appear harmless with a four-year-old toddler, but when that

---

Chapter Summary

We often think we know what our dogs are thinking, but quite often they see a situation entirely differently from how we expect them to. It is easy to influence your dog's likes and dislikes and his moods without realizing it. Always make time for your dog, especially 'quality time'. What you feed your dog is more important than when you feed him, for food can alter performance. Children can benefit from having a family dog, but the commitment must not be taken lightly and, if in doubt, wait.

CHAPTER 10

Living with Your Dog

If it seems like hard work when you are educating your dog or if sometimes you feel like cutting a few corners, think ahead to that wonderful time when you can take your dog anywhere. You be able to share different scenery, training, walks and holidays. Trust me when I say that it is worth that little extra effort and commitment. However, we never stop learning in life and we never stop learning about our dogs, so there is still more to think about.

Jealousy can rear its ugly head at any time, and, if you already have a dog, a new one may appear a threat to it. Similarly, if an additional person is to join your family it can cause jealousy from a dog of any age.

Introducing a New Dog

If you think your first dog may be jealous, make sure that it receives the normal amount of attention, any more will make it feel hierarchy to the new dog and any less will make it feel left out. I do not believe in establishing a pecking order for my dogs for I am in control and, as far as I am concerned, they should appreciate the fact that I feed them and give them attention; if they are going to show jealousy they will have to wait. If you give the first dog a status above that of dog number two, you have given it permission to be the pack leader of that dog. You are the pack leader of both dogs and your dogs will sort out their own pecking order within the pack and do it with minimal fuss, for, if not, you will send them both to their beds. Do not allow the dogs to interchange beds and feed them in a varying order, for if one expects to be fed first it will begin to push the other back. The rules of the pack must be adapted to the house and hostility between the dogs is not allowed. Do not get a second dog to keep the first dog company for it should not need it. If it is lonely, where are you? If you think it would be nice for it to have one of its own kind to play with, you may find that they prefer each other's company to yours. What will have been a good intention could end up with your being just the food supplier and ball thrower. Two dogs are twice the work! It may be lovely to see them on a walk together, but they need to be educated individually and they both deserve quality time separately. They are individuals and this must be nurtured not ignored.

I never advise having two puppies together for it is difficult to individualize them, and they will grow up being dependent on each other rather than on you if you are not diligent with your training and leadership. Try to have at least a six-months gap between them. If you have an older dog and you are introducing a

If you have the facilities to provide your dog with an outside run or play pen it can serve many purposes. Your dog will have his own place in the garden; your children and their friends will not be in his way nor he in theirs and you can bring him in when you have the time to be with him. Floss and Gem share a garden hut with a wire door.

puppy, remember that no dog is perfect and, just as your pup will inevitably develop some bad habits, it will also copy the habits of the older dog, good or bad.

If you are going to have dogs of different breeds it is preferable to aim for breeds that are similar in size and character, as there is a better chance of their complementing each other. Dogs of extreme opposites may be compatible in as much as they will rarely do anything together. For example, a toy or miniature breed will not want to run over the moors with a German Shepherd and it is unlikely that they will play energetic games together. A Border Collie, a retriever, a setter, a German Shepherd and all other breeds noted for their energy can soon physically damage a smaller breed of dog or a puppy if they are allowed to play unsupervised. When children play to the point of overexcitement it can end in tears; when dogs 'overplay' the result may be damaged joints or even a fight.

Introducing a New Person

I know that treats may appear a good standby, but dogs are not fools and the

Or you can build a special run like the one Ross, Alice and Shannie have.

ploy of a 'new person' always being armed with sweets will alert your dog to using manipulative tactics. This often has a way of backfiring and the dog may end up holding the stranger to ransom, with bared teeth, for a packet of biscuits. It is your home and you can have in it whom you like, but, of course, you want them all to get on. Just as with the older dog, do not make too much fuss and do not leave your dog out, but neither must you force him to show an opinion, for it might not be what you want. If the newcomer is an adult discourage them from making advances to your dog, let time take its course; if your dog does not behave acceptably then he must stay in his own 'quarters', but do not force a confrontation. We rarely make friends overnight, we need time, and so does your dog.

If the newcomer is a baby, your dog may be upset by the noise; the constant crying can distress us and we understand it. A dog's hearing is sensitive and he will be under stress with the upheaval so try to remove him from any disturbance if at all possible. If you can give him a place of his own in the garden (it could be a shed with a run) you will all benefit. When the baby is demanding your time or is crying, your dog will be out of the way and amusing himself; when you bring him in for his quality time with you he has no need to be resentful of the new arrival. When the baby is older, your dog will have a retreat where no children are allowed and he will be able to enjoy his privacy; neither will there be a problem at a later date when visiting children are playing in the garden. If you can keep this concept in mind for your dog and your baby in the house, you will give your dog as much of a noise-free zone as possible. Introduce your dog to your baby gently and do not force the issue, if a dog is allowed time to adjust it can be very protective towards children.

Possessive Dogs

Dogs can be possessive over a variety of things: food, toys, bones, other dogs and people. We are back to basics again, for if the handler is the pack leader and has explained the rules carefully, the dog should realize that it does not own anything to be possessive over.

Possessiveness with food can be instinctive with many dogs and in some cases it is inherited from a parent and, although it is not permissible for a dog to be aggressive, I can sympathize with some dogs over the issue of food. If they are provided with a safe eating area where they will not be disturbed, then there is no need for them to be possessive. It is essential that you can take your dog's food from it should the occasion arise; but if you are the pack leader your dog will allow you to take it. When you know that you are in control and you can remove the food when you want, do not ever do it unless it is necessary. If I were a dog and someone kept picking my dinner up and then putting it back down again it would *make* me aggressive. The theory behind such an action is that, should a child pick up the dish, the dog will not bite them. My dogs know they should not bite children and they also know that they are fed in their own quarters, to eat their meal in peace, and that no one but me is likely to disturb them. Should a child venture near a dish, my dogs would come to me and complain. If I am rehabilitating a rescue I make sure that such a situation cannot arise until I have it educated. If, for any reason, I have to remove a full dish that one of my dogs is eating from, I just move it, say 'Sorry, pal', and put it somewhere else for it to finish its dinner. The reaction is usually a placid, 'Okay mum, but did you pinch a bit?' If I have to remove a full dish from a rescue it would be only when we understand each other. I would make sure there that was no element of surprise; I would tell it what I intended to do and then do it. If I thought it would cause a confrontation, I would leave the dish: for me to get bitten or the dog to be made submissive is not the answer. Patience and good timing are essential with problem dogs.

It does not worry me if a dog likes to give itself a sore throat. Skye is such a bossy boots that, the moment her food is put in front of her, she begins warning the world to stay away. Nobody takes any notice, neither I nor the other dogs, because we all know that she is not allowed to carry it any further; but she seems to enjoy it and it is her food that is going cold while she is grumbling, not mine nor the other dogs'. Glen is a sweet-natured, kind dog and at the time of writing is just over one year old; but he was the bossy one of the litter and would have been dominant if I had allowed it. He is well-mannered and very biddable, but he does tend to be a little possessive towards me and I will not allow him to be overprotective. As he is maturing I am being more flexible with him; he does not show a dominant possessiveness just a lovable one, but it must still be controlled.

Socialization

Your dog needs to be socialized, but it can be a big mistake to try and deliberately do it or to do it too soon. First it must identify and respect you as its pack leader and it must have some good manners; if it trusts you it will not feel threatened when it goes out into the wide world. If you take it to a preplanned meeting of dogs and people it can have an adverse affect. Dogs that have been socialized in this way have a preconceived idea that all dogs want to play, and this may eventually cause problems for both dog and handler. If a dog thinks that all dogs are friendly, it will approach every dog it sees. This can lead to aggressive behaviour if it gets rebuffed, and not all dog owners like other dogs to invade their pack space. If a dog develops naturally it will learn to be cautious of other dogs; its instinct will tell it how to behave and what body language to use. If we take away that natural instinct by telling it that all dogs are there for it to play with, it will lose some part of natural dog development. This is the human element making decisions again, and, in their anxiety to ensure that their dog is not aggressive or shy, they risk creating another set of problems.

If a dog is shy or nervous in company it will be looking to you for protection, and if you force it into a situation, such as a training class, before it is ready you may destroy any trust it had in you. Keep the dog away from any threats until it trusts you and then begin to introduce it to people and other dogs slowly and at his pace. Never be pushed into rushing your dog or going against your own instincts. This is your dog, you live with it and you know it best. I never 'socialize' my dogs, they do not go to classes and they do not meet other dogs very often. When I take them for a walk and they see other dogs they are not interested in them; if I go to a sheepdog trial they will, with my permission, mix with the other dogs quite happily. When people come on the Sheepdog Experience my dogs are not shy or nervous; on the contrary, they can be quite cheeky sometimes. If there is another dog in the field they do not take their attention from me, they do not fuss over the other dog and they do not show any aggression towards it. If the other dog shows aggression, and many do, my dogs ignore it and keep out of the way; if the other dog becomes a pest I will give mine permission to put it in its place; this is done with a growl and works first time.

When to Join a Training Class

It is up to each individual if and when they join a class and for what reason. Most of the basic training can be done at home and in the first few weeks; if you join a class and your dog has no recall and does not walk to heel, how have you been managing with him? Trainers are there to help and give guidance, but it is not fair to take an unruly, bad-mannered dog to classes, it is unfair on both the instructor and the other handlers. If your dog has a problem and he is in a class with a lot of

A good dog-training club will have a lot to offer you: basic training, advanced training, competitions and meeting new people.

dogs and people, you may exacerbate the problem before you cure it, so ask the instructor if you and your dog would benefit from one-to-one sessions to begin with. There are some good training clubs with some sensible instructors who teach basic good manners; but some clubs teach the fundamentals of competition work and you do not need this until your dog is under control. When your dog has an instant recall and walks in your pack space, when he is not a nuisance to other dogs and people, then is the time to begin competition training. Do not be persuaded by well-meaning friends to join a club if you do not feel ready, they may be competing with their dogs and yours may only be a youngster. If you feel that you need help with your training then it is sensible to seek it, so look for a good club with a trainer you can understand and who uses methods you like. You took time to choose your dog and you have taken time to educate him, now take time to choose a good training class that suits you both. When you feel ready to go a stage further, it may be more advanced training or you may want to compete in one of the many disciplines, talk to your instructor, for if they do not do the training you are wanting they should be able to advise you of another good club.

Condition Training

Condition training has advantages and disadvantages and it depends whether you are training your dog intentionally or accidentally. If a dog becomes accustomed to behaving under certain conditions it can become accustomed to relating the behaviour only to the condition. Simply explained, many 'problem' dogs mystify their owners by behaving impeccably at a training class but like a hooligan at all other times. These dogs have been hooligans before they started the classes, but they have understood that once a week at a certain time and venue they behave themselves. They do not associate good behaviour on the night with their owner's being their pack leader: you have to be a leader all the time, they simply associate it with a certain condition. But condition training can work to your advantage if you understand it, for when you have trained your dog to behave for you and not as a conditioned response, you can then teach him certain competition moves under circumstances that he will associate only with a competition environment.

Fun or Fear

There are times when we are enjoying ourselves doing human things, but our dogs may be thoroughly miserable; bonfire night can be a dog owner's nightmare. If your dog is frightened by bangs it may be a good idea to play some music or to try to keep him occupied during the worst part of the noise (this applies also to thunder). Whatever happens, keep your body language and voice normal or you will be supporting his fears.

This immediately makes us think of Christmas and of course this brings excitement and different noises. The bang of this cracker will excite a child with the prospect of trinkets and paper hats. To a dog it is a piece of rolled-up paper and it will soon learn to identify it with not only a frightening noise but also a nasty smell of burning after the bang. Try to make sure that what is fun to you is not fear to your dog.

Reagan and Eric are having fun in the water.

Christmas is a time for plenty of people and excitement, there is a different atmosphere and the home changes, your dog can even see you plant a tree inside! If your dog is something of an extrovert he will love it all and probably end up knocking the tree over; but if your dog is not so outgoing it will be unsure of its surroundings. Make sure that it has a safe retreat, if you have a party do not subject it to everyone's advances, they may be friendly but to your dog they will smell of perfume, after-shave and alcohol. Even the most outgoing dog can be shocked if someone pulls a Christmas cracker near it, so think ahead. My dogs love to raid the presents under the tree, and I daren't tell you what one dog thought the tree was for... They enjoy the festivities and we have to keep them away from the almost empty glasses, but, when the house is full of strangers or if crackers are being pulled, I make sure that they are in their own domain.

Not everyone likes dogs, so make sure that yours does not make unwelcome advances to strangers, even dog lovers may draw the line at a strange dog showering them with muddy paws. Sometimes people can be too friendly, approaching

Teach your dog not to jump up uninvited; not everyone likes dogs and even dog lovers will not appreciate muddy hair and feet. Eric is being told that bath comes before cuddle.

your dog determined to molest it whether you like the idea or not. Your priority is to your dog, so stop unwelcome advances and meet your dog's requirements, not those of a stranger.

If a dog is tied up outside a shop it may be a well-mannered, nice-natured animal, but the child that approaches it may not be as nice. Do try to keep an eye on your dog at all times, and this includes competitions, because people tend to think they can send their child up to any dog and stroke it. This is not fair on the dog or its owner, neither is it fair on the child because there is a risk of its being bitten

and, as in many of these cases, the dog was only protecting its space. Parents need to educate their children sensibly about dogs, whether they actually have one or not is irrelevant.

Living with an Older Dog

There is not much you can tell a veteran dog, for it has done it all and seen you in every conceivable mood, good and bad. He knows when to be quiet, when to cheer you up, when you need a hug, he may even allow you to let off steam occasion-

Do be careful if you ever have to leave your dog unattended. Monty is well-behaved and peaceful, but there is no guarantee that any children or adults passing will be as nice. Never leave a dog outside a busy shop or where children are running and screaming.

ally and the 'look' that we reserved specially for him to make sure that he did not misbehave when he was younger is suddenly being returned. Yes, in addition to making us happy he may also make us feel very guilty with just one glance.

Throughout their lives they give us so much and they ask for very little in return, they give love unconditionally, they walk, run, compete and lie quietly whenever we ask and this is something money cannot buy. They deserve that bit extra from us; they deserve to be understood and, for every elderly dog that you have, there is a youngster waiting to learn from your experiences with this dog. So cherish your golden oldies, give them all the quality time you can afford and, when they are gone, remember what they taught you. For they will never be far away and, after all, who else is going to keep an eye on you as diligently as they?

A Wonderful Experience

Your dog may be small, it may be too big to fit in the car or it may be in between, you may want to compete or go fell walking or you may be happiest pottering

This is not 'spot the dog': there is no dog in the picture. This is the road ahead; there are some shady spots but plenty of sunlight shining through. You cannot see what is round the corner so keep your dog under control and keep going forward and enjoying. This is a picture and it is also your life with your dog, tackle the shady spots with common sense and enjoy the sunshine with your wonderful, four-legged friend.

around the garden and just going for a gentle walk. Whatever breed you choose, of whatever age and no matter what you decide to do together, he is yours, you will know him better than anyone else, so you make the rules and the decisions.

The kindness, respect and understanding given by you will bring a return of a loyalty and love that knows no bounds. When you and your dog become a team you will never have to wonder how to teach him for he will show you. You will never stop learning for he will not let you.

You will create an understanding and an empathy that is special to the two of you, you will be able to go anywhere together and you will never tire of each other's company.

At some time, when you are just sitting watching the world go by or the sun setting, look at the dog at your side and remember that he knows everything about you and he never has to forgive you, for you will never be wrong in his eyes. Now isn't that worth those first few weeks of effort?

Problem-Solving Glossary

Aggression

Aggression is used to describe the behaviour of a dog that is liable to bite; but all animals, including human beings, have a natural survival instinct and this can lead to a show of aggression. How these instincts are controlled can determine whether or not a dog will develop aggressive behaviour. Games of tug and the chewing of toys encourage a dog to use its teeth and can be a forerunner to aggression.

Body language

Dogs communicate by body movements and they understand the body language of their own kind. If they do not see familiar body movements in their owner when they enter a new home they will find it difficult to understand what is wanted of them. Quite often people unwittingly give the wrong messages to their dogs and this can cause confusion. Always try to study your dog's movements and translate them into a 'language'.

Foundation training

All dogs need a good, solid foundation of house rules and must learn what is and is not acceptable; all forms of training are made easier if a dog respects its owner and is well-mannered.

Hierarchy

The highest and most revered place in the pack hierarchy is that of leader. If a dog assumes this position over any member of the family, especially of children, it will believe that it has the right to make decisions. This will cause problems as the animal matures, so good manners at an early age are essential to ensure its proper place in the pack.

Hyperactivity

A dog may be hyperactive if it is displaying signs of overexcitement, often shown by barking and chasing. Some breeds are naturally energetic, but hyperactivity is usually manifested by an energy level higher than the normal; often induced by lack of discipline and the dog's pack position, it can be exacerbated by an incorrect diet.

Mental boundaries

Just like children, all dogs must learn what decisions they can make and what decisions must be left to the parent or the pack leader. If a dog is allowed to make all its own decisions it is elevated in the hierarchy; it is important that your dog respects you and is aware of your higher-ranking position.

Mental stimulation

Although exercise is important and will tire the dog physically, mental exercise must not be overlooked. Gentle and quiet games played with a soft ball to make the dog think rather than run will stimulate its mind and will tire it mentally.

Natural space

A dog will consider the area immediately surrounding him as his 'own space' and may react when there is an intruder into it. Some dogs feel naturally protective towards this space and it is important to know how large or small your dog's area is to enable you to avoid any confrontation with him until he has gained confidence and trust in you. To be aware of your dog's space will help to overcome problems with nervousness or aggression.

Nervousness

Some dogs are naturally more introvert than others but most of them can be given confidence with correct handling. Dogs may become insecure if they do not have confidence in their pack leader; this can then manifest itself as nervousness or nervous aggression.

Pack leader

There are only two main positions in the pack: you are either the leader or you are a member of the pack. It is essential that your dog sees you as the pack leader; if you make this quite clear in the first few days you will not find the training of your dog difficult

and he will gain confidence without arrogance.

Physical boundaries

It is important to teach your dog your pack area and to ensure that he knows that he must not leave this area without your permission. This includes not only the house and the garden but also beyond these when you go for a walk, so always keep him in 'your space' until he has learnt to keep focused on you mentally and not just visually.

Quality time

Quality time is the time spent with just you and your dog enjoying each other's company and sharing quiet moments. This time together is essential for creating that special relationship between dog and handler and is important for dogs of all sizes and breeds.

Recall

Every dog, whatever his breed and size, should come back to his owner when he is called and should not have to be called twice. To make sure that your dog learns an instant recall do not allow a situation to develop where you have to repeat your command, and keep him inside your pack area until he respects your commands.

Word association

Dogs do not understand our language; they have to learn certain words and they will connect a word to an action. You must be careful to make sure that you do not keep repeating words or use the same word for two different actions.

Further Information

Useful Contacts

Mainline Border Collie Centre
Freedom of Spirit Magazine
Bingley
West Yorkshire
BD16 3AU
www.bordercollies.co.uk
sykes@bordercollies.co.uk

Kennel Club
1–5 Clarges Street
Piccadilly
London
W1Y 8AB
www.the-kennel-club.org.uk

International Sheep Dog Society
Chesham House
47 Bromham Road
Bedford
MK20 2AA
www.intsheepdogsoc.org.uk

Battersea Dogs Home
4 Battersea Park Road
London
SW8 4AA
www.dogshome.org
info@dogshome.org

RSPCA
Enquiry Service
Causeway
Horsham
West Sussex
RH12 1HG
www.rspca.org.uk

Useful Websites

www.k9netuk.com
General dog information, contacts, books, videos

www.crufts.org.uk
Information on Crufts dog show

www.agilitynet.com
Comprehensive information on agility

www.aspads.org.uk
Information on working trials and *Working Trials Monthly*

Index